Key to Victory

Key to Victory

The Maiden City in the Second World War

Richard Doherty

GREYSTONE

First published in the United Kingdom 1995
Greystone Books Ltd
Caulside Drive, Antrim

ISBN 1 870157 21 4

The Derry City Council Atlantic Memorial Project
is grateful for the financial support of the following
organisations:

Derry City Council
Northern Ireland Tourist Board
Department of the Environment, Londonderry Development Office
The Honourable The Irish Society

Cover: Rodney Miller Associates, Belfast
Printed by W & G Baird Ltd, Antrim

Introduction

WHETHER Derry or Londonderry, the city on the Foyle has a history among the richest on this island. In terms of military history it is arguably the most outstanding, and certainly outshines anywhere else in Northern Ireland.

The city that we know today might not exist but for its military importance in the late-16th century, when it provided a base for English soldiers to create a wedge between the Irish clans of north Ulster. But even before that, the settlement had been touched by matters military: the Vikings had attacked it, and the bloodiest defeat inflicted on those seaborne raiders happened near Derry. After the Plantation of Ulster the city was destroyed by Sir Cahir O'Doherty and later rebuilt as Londonderry with strong walls intended to keep out the Irish clans. Those walls kept out King James II's soldiers in 1689 when the city was the focus of a major European war, a role which was repeated half a century ago and which is the subject of this book.

When the city defied King James its part in his downfall became legendary and is still celebrated in song, story and myth. Yet, during the years of the Second World War, the city played a far more important part in a war on which hinged the future not only of Europe but of much of the western world. Few of its citizens are aware of just how important the city was to the Allied war effort in those years, and to the eventual victory that was gained at such great cost. This book tries to restore the balance to some degree.

There are those who question the value of looking back on any war and who would regard doing so as being introspective and, perhaps, abnormal. Indeed, some would even argue that the Second World War is best forgotten, that it should be confined to the dustbin of history since war is obscene and mankind should be trying to live together in peace. Such arguments may spring from the best of intentions but those intentions are often misguided. To try to forget war, and the lessons of war, is to risk further war: the period between the two world wars of this century serves to underline that point. But the Second World War was unique among wars: it was a war that *had* to be fought, a war in which the Allies were on the side of right, a war with a moral purpose.

The late A J P Taylor, a radical historian, once wrote that no-one who 'rode with the tanks into liberated Belgium or saw the German murder camps at Dachau or Buchenwald could doubt that the war had been a noble crusade'. Taylor's statement underlines the moral purpose of the war which was further underlined by Pope Pius XII who declared that the Allies were fighting a war for 'peace with justice'. Taylor and Pius XII were unlikely to have agreed on many matters; that they were agreed on the moral imperative driving the Allied cause between 1939 and 1945 is simple proof of the breadth of support that that cause enjoyed.The Second World War was won by an alliance that, during 1942, adopted the title United Nations. That alliance was led by three major powers who played the most important parts in the defeat of Nazism, Great Britain, the Soviet Union and the United States of America. It would be wrong to try to argue that any one of those powers was more important than its partners. Each had its particular role to play, and their leadership of the United Nations can be likened to a three-legged stool: remove any leg and the stool will no longer stand. Had any of the three leading partners been removed from the alliance the stool would have collapsed and Fascism would have triumphed.

The United States provided a seemingly inexhaustible supply of war material and manpower; the Soviet Union bled Hitler's forces white and helped make possible the invasion of Europe; Britain's tenacity in 1940, when it stood alone after the fall of France, and its role in the buildup to the invasion were equally vital to Allied success. Part of Britain's role prior to the Normandy invasion was to become a huge ordnance and supply depot for the invasion forces, as well as accommodating those forces. None of this would have been possible without mastery of the Atlantic trade routes which were very nearly wrested from allied control by the unterseebooten, or U-boats, of the German Kriegsmarine.That the U-boats were eventually defeated was due to a number of factors; one very important factor was the strategic position of the port of Londonderry and its availability to the allied navies.

Professor J W Blake, the official historian of Northern Ireland in the Second World War, wrote that

> Londonderry held the key to victory in the Atlantic . . . [as] our most westerly base for repair, the working up and the refuelling of destroyers, corvettes and frigates. . . . By that most critical spring [1943] when the battle for the security of our Atlantic lifelines finally turned our way, Londonderry was the most important escort base in the northwestern approaches . . .

That key role was acknowledged on 14 May 1945 when a token force of eight U-boats made their way under Royal Navy escort into Lough Foyle and upriver to the jetty at Lisahally where the Commander-in-Chief, Western Approaches, Admiral Sir Max Horton took the official surrender. The key had finally been turned.

This book began life as a short account of the city's role in the Second World War but it would be impossible to do true justice to that role in a single volume. As the research process developed it became clear that there were so many facets to the story that a conventional narrative approach would be difficult to sustain.The final format is therefore a compromise between telling the story in an interesting fashion without burdening the reader with too much fine detail and doing justice to the subject.The approach is rather 'bitty' as a result with chapters devoted to what was happening in the city alongside others dealing with what was happening in the Atlantic and elsewhere; I have, for example, chosen not to recount the experiences of many escort groups on the Atlantic run but to encapsulate those experiences through the account written by the late Evelyn Chavasse, DSO, DSC, of his Canadian Group's trip from Newfoundland to Derry in May 1943. I trust that my readers will excuse the style of the book and appreciate the reasons for it.

Richard Doherty

Londonderry Gun Defended Area

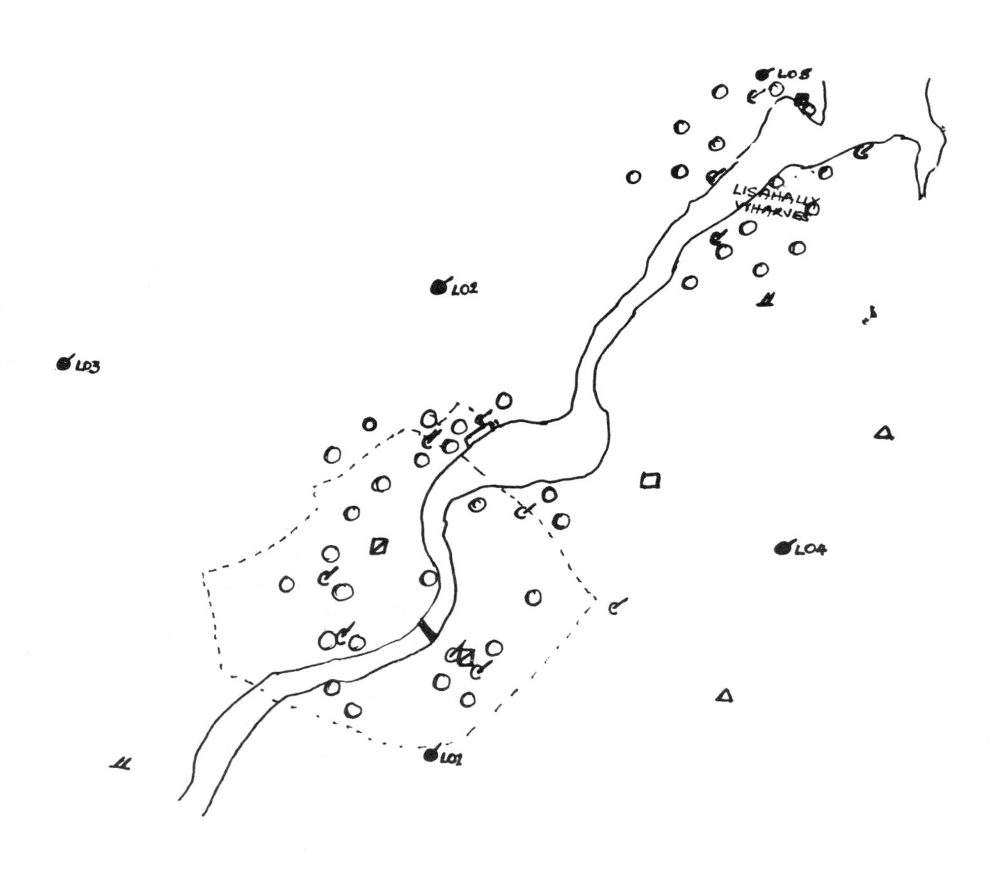

KEY

BALLOON SITE	○
BALLOON SQUADRON HQ	□
BALLOON FLIGHT HQ	⍁
HEAVY AA GUN-SITE	●
LIGHT GUN AA SITE	○
AA ROCKET SITE	//
AMMUNITION DEPOT	△
CITY BOUNDARY	---

1

THE U-BOAT THREAT

The Battle of the Atlantic was one of those battles around which history, and the fate of nations, pivoted. It was a keynote battle that raged from the first until almost the last day of the Second World War in Europe, a total of 2,073 days. While the menace of the German U-boat fleet had been blunted by May 1943, the threat from those submarines did not go away although, after that month, they never wrought the same destruction as before and the hunter increasingly became the hunted.

The fate of the U-boats was almost sealed before the war since Hitler entered a war with an unprepared navy whose 1939 shortfall in equipment was never made good. However, the balance could easily have tipped the other way; Britain was also unprepared for war and it was Britain, her navy and merchant marine that was to bear the greatest burden of the Battle of the Atlantic.

Germany's submarine fleet was limited by treaty restrictions placed on her after the First World War during which a relatively small submarine fleet came close to closing the Atlantic sea lanes from North America. Hitler's Germany ignored those restrictions and secretly built more submarines. In late 1937, Hitler made clear to his service chiefs his intention of going to war with Britain. While his army and air force were superior to their British counterparts, Hitler's navy was weak compared with the Royal Navy. The Führer ordered a committee to investigate how best to build up German naval strength. In early 1938 Hitler was told by that committee that he had two options: construction of a fleet of 'pocket battleships', such as the *Admiral Graf Spee*, and U-boats; or a fleet of major surface ships, battleships and cruisers to rival the Royal Navy. The time scale was critical: the first option involved a relatively short building programme while the second would take a minimum of seven years. But Hitler and Grand Admiral Erich Raeder, the Kriegsmarine's Commander-in-Chief, opted for the second plan, the Z Plan, and a Fleet of 10 battleships, 3 pocket battleships, 2 aircraft-carriers, 16 cruisers, 190 submarines and many destroyers. The fleet would deploy in four groups: one would bottle up the British Home Fleet; a second would strike against merchant shipping; the other two would be fast strike forces supporting the second group.

War came too soon for the Kriegsmarine. In September 1939 the Royal Navy outnumbered its foe 7:1 in battleships, 6:1 in cruisers and 9:1 in destroyers. Only a sixth of the submarine fleet needed to eliminate the British merchant service had been constructed, forcing Raeder to opt for a swift submarine campaign against British shipping. U-boats were in position to strike before Britain declared war on Germany on Sunday 3 September 1939. A signal issued on 19 August advising of a submarine officers' reunion was the code for the U-boats to take up war stations around the British Isles.

On the first evening of war the liner SS *Athenia* was struck by a torpedo off the north coast of Ireland and went down with the loss of 112 passengers and crew, although the majority of the 1418 people on board were rescued. U-30 sank the *Athenia* in contravention of the Submarine Protocol of the London Naval Treaty of 1930, to which Germany had acceded in 1936. Hitler had been anxious that German submarine crews should adhere to this protocol since he did not want to arouse the fury that had greeted the sinking of the *Lusitania* in 1915. He was especially keen not to aggravate France and Britain to whom he intended to put out peace feelers after the subjugation of Poland. However, he gradually approved reductions in restrictions on U-boat engagements until, by November 1939, any ship not clearly marked as neutral could be attacked; and neutral vessels in certain sea areas could also be attacked. Thus unrestricted submarine warfare had arrived by the end of the year.

The Submarine Protocol stated that:

> In their actions with regard to merchant ships, submarines must conform to the rules of International Law to which surface vessels are subject.
>
> In particular, except in case of persistent refusal to stop on being duly summoned, or of active resistance to visit and search, a warship, whether surface vessel or submarine, may not sink or render incapable of navigation a merchant vessel without having first placed passengers, crew and ship's papers in a place of safety. For this purpose, the ship's boats are not regarded as a place of safety, unless the safety of the passengers and crew is assured, in the existing sea and weather conditions, by the proximity of land, or the presence of another vessel which is in a position to take them on board.

Adherence to such rules of engagement would have made an effective submarine campaign against merchant shipping almost impossible. Although accepting the Naval Treaty, Germany added a codicil to the Submarine Protocol clearly defining the individual submarine commander's scope for action.

> As long as war against merchant shipping is governed by the Prize Regulations, attacks are to be aimed at ships which, by the [submarine] protocol, may be sunk without warning. These are:
>
> troopships, ie vessels which are observed to be carrying troops or war material, or which may be identified in other ways;
>
> vessels escorted by enemy warships or aircraft;
>
> vessels taking part in enemy actions or acting in direct support of enemy operations, for example by passing intelligence. Participation in operations is presumed if a merchant ship prepares to resist or takes any action calculated to jeopardise the U-boat.

Adherence to the Prize Regulations was obligatory only if enemy ships were unarmed. Stopping an armed merchant ship could involve exposing a U-boat to the danger of a hit on the boat's pressure hull which could damage her to the extent that diving would be impossible 'and transform her into a slow surface craft of negligible fighting capability'. Clearly, this German interpretation of the protocol allowed ships in convoy, or ships which had reported the presence of German aircraft, submarines or surface vessels, to be attacked without warning. Even within these guidelines, sinking the *Athenia* was an embarrassment to Germany and U-30's captain, Leutnant Lemp, was hardly the most popular man in the country.

Two weeks after the sinking of the *Athenia*, U-29, which had already sunk three British tankers, put two torpedoes into the aircraft-carrier HMS *Courageous* which sank with the loss of almost half its 1,000-man crew. The U-boat escaped even though destroyers escorting the carrier dropped depth charges. A month later Gunther Prien's U-47 sank HMS *Royal Oak* in the Scapa Flow anchorage, with the loss of over 800 lives.

Although German surface ships were also operating against merchant vessels – *Graf Spee* was raiding in the South Atlantic – the principal danger clearly came from submarines. U-boats had a tactical advantage over the Royal Navy whose principal method of detection was the First World War-vintage echo-sounding device, asdic (from the initials of the Allied Submarine Detection Investigation Committee responsible for its invention). But asdic, or sonar in American parlance, had limitations: U-boat commanders found they could escape detection by remaining on the surface where they could also make much better speed. Under cover of darkness a surfaced U-boat was extremely difficult to detect. Another operational problem was loss of asdic contact with the prey in the vital seconds immediately before the attacker's depth charges were dropped over the stern; at this point the submarine would be under the hunter but its precise location could not be known.

To protect merchant shipping the Royal Navy re-introduced a tactic from the First World War when U-boats had created devastation on the merchantmen. This was the convoy system for ships travelling at between 9 and 14.9 knots: the war's first convoy actually sailed for Britain from Gibraltar on 2 September. By mid-September British coastal trade was organised in convoys. (British merchant shipping had come under Admiralty control on 26 August, two days after German forces began massing on Poland's borders.)

At the end of October the Royal Navy claimed to have sunk 18 U-boats since the start of the war. This was an optimistic assessment, as was the First Lord of the Admiralty's speech to the House of Commons just over a week later in which the First Lord, Winston Churchill, claimed that 'we are gaining a definite mastery over the U-boat attack . . . in the end we shall break their hearts'. Churchill's longterm forecast may have been accurate; his contemporary analysis was much mistaken. There was no mastery over the U-boats: it was to be many long months before this happened, and many lives were to be lost before Churchill's words finally came true.

In late November Hitler told his commanders that German efforts were to be concentrated against Britain, 'the leading enemy power' whose defeat was essential for German success. He ordered attacks on British industry by mining and blocking British ports, and attacking shipping. The Führer identified Liverpool, London and Manchester as the most vital target ports since they handled 95 per cent of foreign trade. French ports were not to be attacked unless they were being used to break what Hitler described as 'the siege of England'.

Although 1939's U-boat campaign achieved considerable results it was not nearly as effective as the Kriegsmarine would have liked. Peacetime training, with restrictions on the depths to which boats might dive, had failed to show up many faults, mostly due to bad design or shoddy workmanship. As defective valves and seals, and faulty engine mountings, among others, forced boats to dock for lengthy repairs after their first operational cruises, the number of active U-boats fell away in the closing days of 1939. During that winter many were sealed in harbour by thick ice which allowed some measure of relief to Allied shipping; sinkings continued, however, with dozens of merchant vessels sent to the bottom of the Atlantic in the winter months. Although the first attempt to operate U-boats in a group, or pack, had been tried in October 1939 it had not achieved great success and such operations were not immediately adopted as standard tactics.

The U-boat fleet was diverted to assist operations against Norway in May 1940 and did not return to full operational service in the Atlantic until after Norway's fall. Soon after that, the fall of France allowed the nerve-centre of U-boat operations to move to the west coast of France, giving the boats greater operational flexibility. The Admiralty responded to the establishment of U-boat bases in western France by routing convoys north of Ireland while, in August, Hitler declared a total blockade of the United Kingdom with neutral ships also liable to attack.

The Royal Navy's task was to break Hitler's blockade and allow merchant shipping through to Britain. In performing that task naval efforts were supplemented by the squadrons of RAF Coastal Command, created in 1936, whose role was to protect shipping. However, that protection role had been limited to reconnaissance rather than attacking submarines since the Admiralty complacently believed that anti-aircraft guns on escort ships would see off enemy aircraft while improved asdic devices would allow the Navy to meet the U-boat threat without RAF assistance. Coastal Command was restrained furthermore by the attitude of its own service chiefs who were in thrall to the concept of strategic bombing and thus allowed the Command to become the poor relation in the three great fighting commands of the Royal Air Force. (At no time would this be better illustrated than at the height of the U-boat campaign when the RAF made only a parsimonious allocation of the very-long-range American Liberators to Coastal Command.)

Coastal Command entered the war with aircraft that were largely obsolescent and with limited range so that they could do little more than coastal patrolling. Its aircraft were mainly Avro Ansons, with a range of just over 500 miles, a bomb load of two 100 pounders and an endurance of four and a half hours. There was one squadron of American Lockheed B-14 Hudsons with almost double the Anson's radius of operations and fivefold greater bombload – although the bombs had little effect against submarines – greater endurance and greater speed; 250 Hudsons were on order. Two squadrons of Short Sunderland flying-boats were operational; some biplane flying-boats were still in service. Again the RAF had to turn to the USA to order the Consolidated PBY-5 Catalina flying-boat which had entered US Navy service in 1936 and had much greater range than the Sunderland; the wartime RAF was eventually to obtain more of this American aircraft than of the home-built Sunderland.

By the end of 1939 the Germans had sunk 220 merchant ships (755,531 tons) in the Atlantic for only nine U-boats lost, despite the Royal Navy claim to have sunk twice that number in September and October alone. The clear advantage in the Battle of the Atlantic lay with the U-boats, an advantage that they would press as much as possible in the months and years ahead. Their defeat in the Great War had come about through the use of convoys, co-ordinated efforts from escort ships, aircraft and airships, and technical developments such as asdic. North-west Ireland had played a small but valuable part in that first battle of the Atlantic with a Royal Naval Air Service airship station at Ballyliffin in County Donegal and a US Navy flying-boat base at Ture on Lough Foyle. Defeat of the U-boat in Hitler's war would eventually come about in like manner but it was to be some time before the lessons so painfully learned a generation before were to be applied fully. On this occasion, prior knowledge of enemy intentions through the British Ultra organisation would also play a signal part in final victory. And once again the north-west of Ireland, through the waters of the Foyle, would have its part to play.

2

FRONT-LINE CITY

THE second world war saw Londonderry endure another of the sieges for which the city is renowned. But this was a very different siege with the forces menacing the city at a much greater distance. Modern developments in warfare, however, made distance less important and, although the besiegers were rarely seen, their menace was constant.

The rare occasions on which German forces were seen during the war involved Luftwaffe aircraft flying over; on one such occasion the city suffered its only wartime bombing. Off the north coast of Ireland, however, the real besiegers lurked beneath the Atlantic's waves, determined to cut the lifeline from North America upon which Britain, as an island, depended for survival. That menace from the Kriegsmarine's U-boats placed Derry in the centre of the world stage by making the city's port vital to the Allied war effort. Maintaining ocean links with North America was crucial to the survival not just of the city itself, but of the European continent.

In 1939 nothing indicated that Derry would become the most important naval escort base in the United Kingdom. At the beginning of the war, the Admiralty actually believed that the Treaty ports of Berehaven, Cobh and Lough Swilly, handed back to the Dublin government in 1938, would be available to the Royal Navy. Lough Swilly, the major naval base in the north-west of Ireland during the First World War, would have been so again, had Dublin made it available. That the Admiralty expected to be using those ports is demonstrated by a note in an Admiralty file regarding the posting of a Royal Navy Volunteer Reserve officer, Paymaster Lieutenant-Commander OW McCutcheon, in September 1939. McCutcheon was appointed to the staff of the Naval Officer-in-Charge, Buncrana, but, pending resolution of the Treaty Ports' situation, would report to the staff of the Flag Officer-in-Charge, Belfast. Needless to say, McCutcheon was never based at Buncrana.

Soon after war began a British Expeditionary Force arrived in France to support the French army. Many believed that the ground war in Europe would be a repeat of the First World War with trench warfare dominating. The Germans had other ideas and, in May 1940, launched a major offensive against French and British forces, ignoring Dutch and Belgian neutrality in doing so. French army morale was poor and many French formations crumbled in the face of their enemy. Those that remained intact, together with the BEF, Belgian and Polish troops, held the Germans long enough for most of the BEF, with large numbers of French and other allied troops, to escape from France.

In June 1940 the French government sued for an armistice. France was out of the war and Britain stood alone. Opposing Britain across the channel was the greatest power the European continent had ever seen but, led by the new prime minister, Winston Churchill, the country determined to fight on. More than ever the Atlantic shipping lanes became Britain's lifeline; the neutral United States had become Britain's arsenal.

With most of France occupied the Germans were able to begin construction of U-boat bases in France; U-boat headquarters moved from near Wilhelmshaven to Paris for a short time and then to Kerneval, near Lorient, in Brittany where a command centre was established.

> Officers had been sent to France early in June, to select suitable bases for U-boats. On the day of the armistice . . . torpedoes, air-compressors, torpedo stores and personnel were sent by road from Wilhelmshaven to Paris and onwards for distribution among these bases. It was desirable at once to clear a U-boat route through the Channel and off the proposed German bases in France. There were only sufficient minesweepers to clear the approaches to Lorient and this was immediately put in hand.

Rear-Admiral Karl Dönitz, the U-boat Commander-in-Chief, inspected the Atlantic coast of France and recommended that bases be developed in stages, as follows:

a/ supply facilities for weapons, fuel and provisions
b/ facilities for short repairs
c/ the transfer of the U-boat Command to the west as soon as (a) and (b) were available for the Atlantic boats
d/ facilities for complete overhaul of U-boats

On 7 July, U-30 became the first boat put into Lorient to refuel and replenish its torpedoes after an Atlantic voyage. Within a month Lorient's dockyard was handling U-boat repairs, a task it performed more efficiently than German dockyards. France became home to the submariners and French ports, such as Brest, Lorient, St Nazaire, La Pallice and Bordeaux, removed the necessity for a long voyage around the British Isles. The new bases saved time as well as mileage as, hitherto, areas of the North Sea, Skagerrak and Kattegat had to be crossed at night under escort. As Dönitz himself noted in his Memoirs

> . . . they were saving something like a week on each patrol and were thus able to stay considerably longer in the actual area of operations. This fact, in turn, added to the total number of U-boats actively engaged against the enemy.

The French ports acted as a 'force-multiplier', greatly increasing the danger to merchant shipping in the Atlantic. And, whereas the original U-boat bases had presented greatest threat to shipping in the north-western approaches, north of Ireland, these new bases made the south-western approaches more vulnerable causing convoys to be routed around the north coast of Ireland to have the best chance of evading the German submarines. The Royal Navy needed a base as far west as possible as a repair and refuelling facility for convoy ocean escorts. That called for a port in north-west Ireland. For the Admiralty, deprived of Lough Swilly, Captain Philip Ruck-Keene identified the Foyle and the port of

Londonderry as a suitable base which would extend the range of ocean escorts by 100 miles. Towards the end of the First World War, the US Navy had briefly had a flying-boat base at Ture on Lough Foyle and some ship repair work had been carried out in the city, but Londonderry had never before been a major naval base.

Its possible use by the Royal Navy in 1940 was complicated by the Irish government's attitude towards British warships in what Dublin considered Irish waters. It seemed that London also believed the tidal waters of the Foyle, and its estuary, to be Irish, under the terms of the Treaty, for in August 1940 the Director, Anti-Submarine Warfare wrote to the Admiralty emphasising the need to base anti-submarine strike forces as far west as possible on Ireland's north coast. The Director wrote that the Flag Officer-in-Charge, Belfast had reported that the Irish authorities had no objection to Royal Navy use of 'Londonderry and Lough Foyle as a base provided we go ahead and do so without referring the matter to the Free State authorities'. The Irish compromise was, therefore, one of being unable to refuse a request that was not made. Paradoxically, Article 6 of the Treaty made the Royal Navy responsible for the waters around Ireland; Article 7 covered the Treaty Ports, one of which was Belfast.

In August the depot ship HMS *Titania* arrived in Derry while 3rd Motor Launch (ML) Flotilla was transferred from Coleraine to the city; the first Royal Navy warship to tie up in the port had been HMS *Notts County* on 10 June 1940. In September, Captain Ruck-Keene was appointed Naval Officer-in-Charge, Londonderry and, on 16 October, he proposed that a maintenance and repair base be established in the city; refuelling facilities on the river for escort ships were already planned. Those facilities included constructing a naval dockyard at Pennyburn and lengthening, by forty-five feet, the old graving dock. At the time it was noted that 'repair facilities in Derry may be of priceless value next summer'. By the end of the year 3rd ML Flotilla had been joined by 1st and 2nd Escort Groups, deploying fifteen ships in total, of which eight were destroyers, and a nominal base ship had been commissioned; *Titania* had been replaced by HMS *Sandhurst*. Anti-submarine exercises off the north coast had resulted in Coastal Command officers being appointed to the Londonderry Naval Headquarters.

The new base ship was the yacht *Firefly*, now renamed HMS *Ferret*, which was moored in the Foyle. Although the name HMS *Red Branch*, with obvious Irish connections, had been proposed, *Ferret*, first used as a ship's name in 1704, was chosen instead. (A popular local belief that Ebrington Barracks was taken over completely by the Royal Navy and renamed HMS *Sea Eagle* during the war is not accurate; *Sea Eagle* did not come into being until HMS *Ferret* decommissioned in 1947. In late 1940 Ebrington Barracks was still an Army establishment; not until mid-1941 was any part of Ebrington handed over to Admiralty control.)

As well as lengthening the graving dock, many other harbour facilities were expanded and new facilities created. Harland and Wolff built a large repair workshop; a coaling station was set up; a boiler-cleaning party was sent to the city; fourteen destroyer berths were built on the west bank of the Foyle in the city with three minesweeper berths on the east bank; a motor launch slipway was constructed; and a forty-seven acre ammunition dump was built at Kilnappy.

Talbot House was requisitioned to be used as a HQ and sick quarters. (Later it was adapted, splinter-proofed and extended as an operational headquarters for the US Navy, the Oaks House replacing it as a naval sick quarters; in 1943, Magee College was requisitioned as the RN headquarters for escort ships operating from the Foyle). But the major feature of the Admiralty programme was the building of a 2,300 feet long jetty at Lisahally, with a depth of eighteen feet of water alongside, and connected to the shore by three piers. Along the jetty ran a two-foot gauge railway which opened in 1943.

Throughout 1941 further naval units arrived, while 6th ML Flotilla replaced the 3rd Flotilla. (The motor launches were transferred to the Nore command on the south-east coast of England on 19th April 1941.) Among the new arrivals were a dozen trawlers converted for anti-submarine warfare. By the end of 1941 eleven escort groups were operating from Derry on the arduous task of protecting convoys from North America. The base had outstripped Liverpool and Greenock in importance and could handle 110 escorts.

In the early months of the war few escort ships were available and the burden fell mainly on Great War vintage destroyers such as the V and W Class vessels which were not really suitable for this work. After the Norwegian and French campaigns, during which the Royal Navy lost many destroyers, the situation worsened and led to convoys sailing with minimal escorts, as destroyers were held back in home waters as a precaution against a German invasion. Derry-based escort vessels were also assigned an anti-invasion role as there were expectations that such operations might be in Irish waters with the Shannon estuary a probable enemy landing site.

A frantic building programme had begun to produce sloops and corvettes as escort vessels but the fruits of this programme were slow in coming through as peak production had yet to be achieved. Against this background British bases in the Caribbean were 'traded' for vintage American destroyers in August, while U-boat crews were enjoying their 'happy time', that period from July to October 1940 when they could operate almost at will in the Atlantic. Only in those months, and in the second 'happy time' off the American coast in 1942, according to a German naval source, 'did the men of the U-boat arm feel entirely equal to the enemy defences'.

The backbone of convoy escorts was to be composed of Flower-class corvettes, originally designated as sloops for coastal work. These little ships were adapted from a whalecatcher design. The Flowers had the advantage of manoeuvrability but their short length made them extremely lively and wet, which made the crews extremely uncomfortable; serving on a Flower was an exhausting occupation. Although the class was modified to make it more tolerable for ocean work, its speed was less than that of a surfaced U-boat so it could not be used to chase such boats.

In the winter of 1941/42 escorts worked in relays across the Atlantic, since none had the fuel capacity to take a convoy the entire way across the ocean while manoeuvring around a convoy to deter or attack U-boats. Normally a homebound convoy was collected by its escort south of Newfoundland at the Western Ocean Meeting Point, or Westomp, and taken to the Mid-Ocean Meeting Point, Momp, where a western approaches escort, generally from Londonderry, would take over. The released escort then went to Iceland to refuel and came out to meet another western approaches escort with an outbound convoy at the Momp. Fuelling was critical: the problems caused by lack of 'legs' prevented convoy routes being moved further south to avoid adverse weather conditions and U-boat concentrations. Escorts often had to leave a convoy early, greatly increasing the risk to the convoy's ships. In 1942 trials were undertaken off the north Irish coast involving ships from the Londonderry Escort Force in ship-to-ship refuelling and, in June, refuelling of escorts from tankers was introduced.

Refuelling at sea allowed better evasive routing of convoys. At much the same time British and Canadian ships took over most Atlantic escort work to release US Navy ships to protect US coastal convoys, cover the North African landings, and for the Pacific war. US coastal shipping had suffered heavily at the hands of a mere 21 U-boats. Roosevelt's government had refused to allow a blackout of the Florida coast so as not to harm civilian morale, nor did they institute a convoy system: the result was the loss of 505 ships, many of them just off the Florida beaches.

From mid-1942, Royal Canadian Navy ships escorted convoys between New York and the Halifax Ocean Meeting Point (Homp) at about 61 degrees West. From there other ships, operating between the Halifax meeting point and Westomp took over for the 'long, grim sub-infested ocean passage', normally covered by British or Canadian ships based on St John's, Newfoundland – the 'Newfie-Derry run' – or, if available, by American escort groups based on Argentia. US-escorted convoys from Iceland might be met at the Iceland Ocean Meeting Point (Icomp) but the ocean escorts normally carried on to the Eastern Ocean Meeting Point, Eastomp, near the Isle of Oversay in the north-western approaches. There a 'local British escort took over and the ocean escort went into Londonderry to prepare for the return passage with an outbound convoy'.

This remained the general pattern of escort operations. From late-1942 when sufficient ships became available to supplement the work of the escort groups, Support Groups were formed to go rapidly to the aid of a convoy threatened by U-boats: the support group would strengthen the convoy's normal escort to drive off the U-boats and then, while the escort sailed on with the convoy, would hunt the submarine or submarines to destruction. Perhaps the most famous of all support group commanders was Captain Johnnie Walker who commanded the first group from September 1942; Walker's group had destroyed 16 boats by the time of his sudden death in July 1944. With the addition of very long range air cover from shore-based aircraft and local air cover from planes carried on small aircraft carriers converted from merchant ships (MAC ships, or Merchant Aircraft Carrier ships) which sailed with convoys and the technical developments that came with them, such as 'Hedgehog' which threw a pattern of depth charges ahead of the ship, the U-boats were on the run from May 1943 onwards.

3

ACTION STATIONS

THE increasing importance of Londonderry's naval base raised the north-west's strategic importance to the highest level with all three services heavily involved in the area. Before the war Coastal Command had identified a site at Aghanloo near Limavady for a base while, in 1940, sites at Eglinton and Ballykelly were earmarked as airfields for Coastal Command, although Eglinton was later allocated to Fighter Command for the defence of Londonderry.

Occupation of France not only gave the German navy bases on the Atlantic seaboard from which to harass merchant shipping, it also provided the German air force, the Luftwaffe, with bases from which to strike against targets in Britain. In the summer of 1940 the Luftwaffe's main thrust was in daylight raids on targets in England, with attacks on Scotland from Scandinavian bases. However, the Admiralty feared that, inevitably, German attention would be turned to Northern Ireland and, particularly, Londonderry. The city needed air defence which involved the Army and Royal Air Force; thus the redesignation of Eglinton as a fighter airfield. Another airfield at Maydown, planned as Eglinton's satellite, was also handed over to Fighter Command.

The Army's part was to provide anti-aircraft (AA) artillery. In September 1940 construction began on gunsites at Corrody, also referred to as Tamneymore, and Galliagh. Gunners of 315 Heavy AA Battery arrived on 9 September and the first guns, at Galliagh, were 'ready for action' on 17 September. Each site accommodated two 3.7-inch heavy anti-aircraft (HAA) guns initially. As there was, as yet, no gunlaying radar for the city, the guns were to be controlled from the RAF Sector Operations Room (SOR) at Aldergrove and could only go into action with barrage fire. Corrody was identified as site LO (for Londonderry) 1, while Galliagh was LO2. Four HAA guns for a strategically important city seems niggardly but must be seen in the light of the Luftwaffe offensive against British cities. AA guns were at a premium: pre-war scales of provision laid down by Anti-Aircraft Command had been vastly increased as war went on with frantic demands for additional guns from cities and bases throughout the UK and overseas. Although industry was working all out to satisfy the demand there were insufficient guns to go round.

As well as fighter aircraft, the RAF also provided a balloon barrage. In October 1940, No.920 Balloon Barrage Squadron transferred from Skye to the city. Within two weeks sixteen balloon sites were in operation and the silver blimps became a familiar sight in the local sky. The first element of the squadron to arrive in Derry was A Flight Headquarters which established itself in the

Brandywell Showgrounds on 4 October; the remainder of the Flight arrived next day. Flight Headquarters soon moved to the old Watts Distillery building in William Street where it remained until 920 Squadron disbanded in 1943.

Squadron Headquarters was established at Cooke's House, Caw, while B Flight had its headquarters near Corrody. The balloon barrage formed a rough circle around the city with sites 1 to 6 east of the Foyle and sites 7 to 16 west of the river. Its purpose was to force attacking bombers to fly higher, thus giving the anti-aircraft guns more time to engage.

On 25 October 1940 the city had its first air-raid warning, followed by two more next day. Although it was mid-December before there was another alert, the Germans were photographing the port with high-flying reconnaissance aircraft. On 9 January 1941, No.920 Squadron noted gunfire to the east and an unidentified aircraft flying eastward. Another high-flying plane was spotted on the afternoon of 18 February. In each case the Luftwaffe machines were too high for the AA guns to engage.

In March 1941 a review of the gun defences was carried out at Admiralty request: four more gunsites were authorised for the Londonderry Gun Defended Area (GDA). Each new site, LOs3, 4, 5 and 6, was to be equipped with four 3.7-inch guns while the original sites were to have their complement increased to match. Production delays had been caused by modifications to the design of the 3.7 and bomb damage to a Royal Ordnance factory producing the guns in Sheffield. As an interim measure, in April, four guns were to be transferred from Cardiff's defences to Derry to bring the city's GDA up to battery level of eight weapons. Before those additional 3.7s arrived the city was bombed by the Luftwaffe.

At 11.40pm on Easter Tuesday, 15 April, air-raid warnings sounded again. To many, this sound was now simply a nuisance and was ignored: they had heard the sirens before when nothing had been seen to happen; this time would be no different. But this warning was followed not by a reconnaissance machine but a bomber, acting on the information built up by the earlier recce flights. The bomber, a Heinkel He111 or a Junkers Ju88, had come from a force sent to bomb Clydeside and Belfast. Most of the bombers had taken off from western France; it is likely that the plane which arrived over Derry at ten minutes before midnight had flown from Vannes in Brittany.

LO1 and LO2 sites, manned by 355 HAA Battery since 19 March, fired three rounds each in a 'Pillar Barrage' at heights from 1,000 feet to 11,000 feet. The intruder, flying at about 8,000 feet, dropped a number of what were described as incendiary devices but were probably flares – the RAF noted these as being red, white and green – and two aerial landmines; the latter were intended for the Pennyburn naval yard. Suspended on parachutes the mines were barostatically detonated to explode at or above ground level, creating maximum blast damage to lightly-built dockyard buildings.

The mines missed their intended target and floated north-westward. One exploded in a sandpit near the Lough Swilly railway station, close to St Patrick's Church on Buncrana Road. This device caused some damage to the church, including allegedly blowing the hand off a statue of St Patrick; local legend soon credited the saint with turning the bomb away from the church.

Unfortunately, no supernatural intervention was placed in the way of the second landmine which exploded at Messines Park causing widespread devastation. Emergency services were soon in operation; RAF men from No.7 balloon site at Pennyburn, 400 yards from the scene, and soldiers from 9th Warwicks at Belmont Camp rushed to assist casualties.

Five houses had been demolished and the operations' record book of 920 Squadron noted that seventeen people had been killed. However, only thirteen bodies were recovered at the time, although another was found several months later by American personnel working on a development project.

Many homes were so badly damaged that 150 people were homeless but Derry's tragedy paled alongside Belfast's travail that night: the latter had suffered the greatest single night's death toll of any city in the UK outside London during the war. Although over 700 people were officially reported killed, the true death toll may have been over 900.

At the time, and for many years afterwards, the German bombing of Derry was described as random and indiscriminate. In his book *The Blitz – Belfast in the war years*, Brian Barton quotes a civil defence report to this effect which, he states, was supported by Naval authorities in the city. In fact, the attack was not indiscriminate, although it is easy to see why the authorities would have subscribed publicly to the view that the city had been hit by a stray bomber. Those authorities knew that a major attack on Derry was probable, especially as the Luftwaffe was now targeting ports. Easter Tuesday's raid could have been an indicator of things to come but a major attack was now unlikely before the winter of 1941/42 since longer daylight hours made night operations against targets in Northern Ireland and Scotland much too risky.

Another theory advanced by Barton, and by Jonathan Bardon, in his *History of Ulster*, is that the German bomber was trying to block the Foyle channel. This appears plausible but, had this been the case, the aircraft would have dropped its bomb load further north from the city as the channel at Pennyburn was much too narrow for accurate targeting from 8,000 feet. Destroying or damaging repair facilities was more likely to disrupt naval operations from the Foyle than dropping two mines into the river which minesweepers would have swept up almost immediately. Another suggestion, that two further mines were dropped in the Foyle, can be dismissed: no German bomber could carry four such weapons from Brittany to Derry, nor were mines found in the river by the minesweepers; an Admiralty report in 1943 which made this clear also questioned the need for a minesweeping service in the Foyle.

On the night of the raid there were no RAF fighters to defend the city. Although a headquarters staff had moved into RAF Eglinton the runways were incomplete; not until August did operational aircraft arrive. Paradoxically, these were Coastal Command Hudsons: ten of No.53 Squadron's aircraft operated from Eglinton for a time that month. The first fighters came in September when Hurricanes of No.504 Squadron from Ballyhalbert were detached for convoy escort duties. On 8 October 1941 No.504 Squadron was relieved by No.133 with Spitfires. This was a special RAF squadron: its flying crews were Americans who, frustrated by their nation's continuing neutrality, had volunteered to fight for Britain. No.133 was one of three 'Eagle' squadrons in the RAF, each composed of American volunteers. As such, 133's Eagles were the first Americans to serve in uniform in Derry during the war, although by the time of their arrival many of their fellow-countrymen were also in the city in civilian clothes while two high-ranking US officers had visited the area on 6 June 1941 and had inspected LO2 gunsite.

Following the Easter Tuesday raid there were further reviews of the defences, especially in view of increased naval activity in the Foyle and the establishment of the new Lisahally anchorage. There had been further Luftwaffe overflights, including one from Donegal on 5 May, the bomber having dropped its bombs near Malin. On 3 July 1941 the Chiefs of Staff (AA) Shadow Sub-Committee

> considered the protection for the proposed Naval base at Lishally [sic] near Londonderry in Northern Ireland. It was agreed to invite the Air Ministry to consider the provision of an additional 24 balloons, in order to extend the Londonderry barrage, to provide protection for the Lishally base.

Sixteen new balloon sites were established under C and D Flights, 920 Squadron, at Culmore and Lisahally respectively, on 18 July with another eight sites for the city being established five days later. The balloon barrage was now forty strong. Although it had been hoped that some balloons might be anchored on barges in the river at Lisahally as a more effective deterrent a shortage of vessels precluded this.

The planned increase in anti-aircraft gunsites was also underway with the opening of site LO3 behind Sheriff's Mountain, close to the Donegal border. LO4 was constructed at Mabuoy, LO5 at Culmore and LO6 at Campsie. Sites LO1 to LO4 formed a box for the port while LO5 and LO6 were to defend Lisahally. As well as the additional heavy guns, Bofors 40mm light anti-aircraft (LAA) guns were added to the local defences during July: eight were allocated to the city docks with another four emplaced to cover Lisahally; this brought a battery of light guns to the area.

A Gun Operations Room was also to be opened at Londonderry: on 24 June Headquarters, 12th AA Division, in Glasgow, with overall responsibility for Northern Ireland's gun defences, ordered 3rd AA Brigade in Northern Ireland to requisition 'forthwith' a house east of the Foyle to accommodate a GOR and a regimental headquarters (RHQ). The Manor House at Eglinton was identified and Londonderry GOR was established there: RHQ, 111th HAA Regiment, responsible for the defence of the city, also moved in on 5 August. As well as controlling all guns in the area, the GOR also co-ordinated with balloons and aircraft. Such co-ordination became more important as the city's defences expanded; one method of achieving this was the creation of an Inner Artillery Zone (IAZ) in which guns had precedence and movement of friendly aircraft was restricted or, at times, banned completely.

Additional LAA guns under Londonderry GOR control were to be based at Magilligan and RAF Limavady. LAA guns were all sited individually; the best-remembered of those in the city was located on the roof of Bryce and Weston's Richmond Factory on Strand Road. These guns were manned by soldiers of 176 LAA Battery which was based in St Columb's House in the Waterside to where, on 30 September, the Battery's HQ transferred from Belfast. The battery's advance party had arrived at St Columb's House on 19 September. A further HAA site, LO7, was authorised for Magilligan Point under control of Londonderry GOR bringing the total of heavy guns defending the city to 28.

The Royal Artillery's final addition to the local AA defences was the establishment, in February 1942, of two rocket sites, one (LOZ 1) at Enagh and the other (LOZ 2) at Ballougry, each with a four-barrel AA rocket launcher. At the end of 1942 the Navy added the anti-aircraft guardship HMS *Foxglove* to the defences with its complement of light AA guns, 20mm and 2-pounder 'pompoms'. With a further twelve light guns and forty balloons, the city's defence assets were, proportionately, greater than those of almost any UK city outside London. Such was the strategic value of the city on the Foyle.

That strategic value was increasing even more. In early 1941 the US government's Lend-Lease Act allowed the supply of war equipment to Britain without payment provided the equipment was returned to the USA when the war ended; payment would be due on any equipment retained after the war. Roosevelt had persuaded Congress that the Act was vital to British survival and the eventual freedom of Europe. Its introduction was most timely: Britain had all but exhausted her gold and currency reserves in buying American weapons and equipment.

Lend-Lease allowed the US to arrange with Britain for the construction of several bases, the largest of which were at Londonderry and at Rosneath, near Glasgow, known as Base I and Base II respectively. The US was also to build. for the British services, flying-boat bases at Lough Erne and at Loch Ryan in Scotland, known as Base A and Base B.

> Financed by the Lend-Lease Act, work began on the construction of these bases in the summer of 1941, and was well on its way by the time the United States entered the war. These bases were chiefly designed to serve ships protecting the movement of convoys in the North Atlantic, and were thus of a defensive nature.

Base I was to be at Lisahally where work was already underway on the construction of the Royal Navy jetty. An Admiralty letter on preparations for US Naval and Army co-operation with British Naval forces noted that there would also be flying-boat operations from Lough Foyle (Londonderry). The United States Navy had clearly not forgotten their use of Naval Air Station, Lough Foyle in 1918. Nothing came of this proposal although the RAF had used the Foyle as a temporary base in the 1930s. (For a time during the War an RAF flying-boat depot ship, the *Manela*, was anchored off Moville but no record of operational use has been found.) In the same Admiralty letter the writer pointed out that construction of the new bases would be carried out by US contractors, supervised by US engineers, with unskilled labour recruited from within the British Isles, 'including Éire'. Although materials were to be shipped from the USA, liability for all labour charges was accepted by the British government.

The first overt sign of American presence in the city came on 30 June when 400 US personnel arrived by ship in the city. Because the USA was still neutral all wore civilian clothes; many were so brightly dressed that onlookers at first thought there were women in the contingent. The technicians were moved to Ebrington Barracks to be accommodated in J, H, B and NO Blocks as well as the Sergeants' Mess; 2nd/7th Warwicks arranged reception and feeding of the Americans until their quarters could be handed over to the Admiralty on behalf of the US Navy. Those quarters had been vacated on 24 June by two companies of Warwicks who moved to a tented camp at Ballykelly.

The work of the Americans was not restricted to Lisahally. A radio communications station; a ship repair facility, capable of servicing and repairing naval vessels, principally destroyers; an ammunition dump; a supply depot of approximately 160,000 square feet; a fuel tank farm of 200,000 barrels of fuel oil, 30,000 barrels of diesel oil, and 30,000 barrels of aviation fuel; a 600-bed hospital; camps for 5,000 personnel; and an administrative headquarters were also to be built. Another 416 technicians arrived on 26 July, followed by groups of 150 and 211 on 1 September and 19 October respectively; many moved on to other locations in Northern Ireland or Scotland. Material was also arriving at the port with 300 Nissen huts being onloaded on 18 July.

The changed face of Londonderry in mid-1941 prompted the Army to propose a major change in the area's administration. Until then the Commander, 182 Infantry Brigade, had carried out the duties of Officer Commanding Troops, Londonderry, assisted by a Garrison Adjutant, a post created in December 1940. This system had worked well in co-ordinating and controlling administrative and amenities' matters and 'was becoming increasingly useful in view of the increasing numbers of Naval, Air Force and other personnel arriving in the city'.

> For operational reasons, however, it has become necessary for the H.Q. of 182 Infantry Brigade to move . . . [and] the Commander . . . will no longer be able to carry out these station duties. Simultaneously the size of the Military Garrison in Londonderry is being reduced and the Senior Officer present will shortly be the OC, the Infantry Battalion in Belmont Camp, which lies west of the river on the Northern outskirts of the city. In view of the growing importance of Londonderry itself, from the Naval point of view, and to some extent also, from the Air Force point of view, it is considered that this function of Station Commander and co-ordinating authority between the Services can no longer be carried out by the Senior Military officer at the station.

The Army recommended that the duties should be assumed by a naval officer 'senior enough for his decisions to carry weight where conflicting questions arise'. The city's image as a naval base was now firmly planted in every mind and that base was beginning to burgeon in size with Ruck-Keene a most enthusiastic commander. In a report entitled 'Expansion of Londonderry Base', dated 3 May 1941, he wrote that

> Unless the enemy captures Southern Ireland, Londonderry will remain, throughout the war, the furthest port from enemy air bases. It will always be the nearest base to the 'Battle of the Atlantic'. The 'Battle of the Atlantic' is the crux of the war and even if this battle is won in the near future it will certainly continue to be a hard struggle until the end of the war. Londonderry will therefore remain of the highest importance throughout the war.
>
> The Lisahally scheme, together with the new dolphins, which are nearly finished, will bring the capacity of the port for operational purposes up to approximately 110 destroyers and corvettes*; this means that over 12,000 men will be based on the port.

That capacity meant that further expansion was required, and among the developments requested by Ruck-Keene was a second dry-dock. When the US

* 68 Royal Navy destroyers and corvettes; 42 US Navy destroyers.

Captain Philip Ruck-Keene who identified the Foyle as a suitable anchorage from escort ships and subsequently became first Naval Officer In Charge, Londonderry. (IWM: A14931)

Karl Donitz, commander of the U-boat service and second Fuhrer of the Third Reich. (IWM: A14899)

An AW Whitley of No.502 (Ulster) Squadron over the Atlantic. The squadron operated Whitleys from Limavady. (IWM: CH7049)

Construction of the US Navy's hospital at Creevagh in very muddy conditions in January 1942. (IWM: A9593)

The destroyer USS *Dallas* is cheered by the British sailors as she arrives in Londonderry in January 1942. the *Dallas* was one of the first US warships to arrive at the port. (IWM: A9198)

Nations united. The White Ensign and the Old Glory fly side by side at Londonderry where British and US warships lie alongside each other at the end of January 1942. (IWM: A9206)

The crew of the 4-inch gun of the Canadian corvette HMCS *Chambly* in port in October 1943. Note the gun crew's artwork (IWM: A20003)

HMS *Duncan*, of 7th Escort Group, on 7 November 1943 after the Group had sunk two U-boats in the North Atlantic. The *Duncan* is watched by men of the corvette HMS *Sunflower* (IWM: A20153)

Sailors of 7th Escort Group walk along the quay carrying sacks containing wooden structured remains of the two U-boats sunk by the Group. (IWM: A20154)

Ships of 7th Escort Group tied up after the sinking of the two U-boats. The group includes HMS *Versatile* (nearest camera) and (from L to R in background) HMIS *Godavari*; HMS *Vanessa*; HMS *Vidette* and HMS *Rochester*. (IWM: A20155)

The german Submarin-Boys thank
the Commanding Officer, the Officers,
and the men of
H.M.S. „Byard"
for all Times
Sinking of the Atlantic 17th Oct 43

Peter Voss
Gerhard Schwerin
Horst Witt
Richard Eder
Reinhard Günther

Gratitude. An illuminated address to the officers and men of HMS *Byard* from the crew of a U-boat which had been sunk by *Byard* and its crew rescued by the British ship. (IWM: A20156)

Lieutenant Pritam Singh Mahindee, RINR, from Amritsar in the Punjab, the navigating officer of HMIS *Godavari*, a Royal Indian Navy ship in the 7th Escort Group, takes a bearing on the bridge of his vessel. The large building in he background is the Richmond Factory on Strand Road, now a supermarket, on the roof of which was mounted a Bofors 40mm anti-aircraft gun. The gun position is to the right of the photograph. (IWM: A20005)

Commodore G W G Simpson, CBE, Commodore (D) Western Approaches in his office at magee College in September 1943. Simpson had arranged the requisitioning of most of Magee in order to rationalise the locations of his headquarters. (IWM: A20736)

Such charmed existence did not follow every ship. USS *Leopold* (DE-319) was escorting a 27-ship convoy on 8 March 1944 when she made contact with a U-boat. This caused the convoy's course to be altered. At 7.50pm next day, south of Iceland, *Leopold* reported a radar contact at 8,000 yards; the 'contact' was, therefore, seven miles south of the convoy. Both *Leopold* and USS *Joyce* (DE-317) were sent to intercept. A U-boat was spotted submerging and *Leopold's* gun crews strove to engage it. Only a few rounds had been fired when *Leopold* was rocked by an explosion: another U-boat, lying in wait off the port quarter, had torpedoed her. The destroyer lost all electrical power and the order was given to abandon ship. Then the stricken vessel broke in two and the fore part was lost. Some survivors were left on the stern which was sinking deeper and deeper in the water. *Joyce* was unable to pick up survivors as there were still at least two U-boats in the vicinity, one of which was firing torpedoes at her. Eventually the stern of *Leopold* turned over on its side and many men, including the captain, Commander Kenneth Phillips, were thrown into the freezing water. When the survivors were finally picked up, there were only 28 of the ship's enlisted men from a complement of 158; all *Leopold's* 13 officers had perished.

Another DE to suffer at the hands of a U-boat was USS *Donnell* (DE-56). On 3 May 1944, while on convoy escort duty, *Donnell* was hit by a torpedo. The submarine was located and engaged by USS *Hopping*, also of the escort division, while the convoy steamed on. Eventually Royal Navy vessels took over and finished off the U-boat as *Hopping* took the badly-damaged *Donnell* in tow. After two days in rough seas British rescue vessels relieved Hopping of her task and the escort division sailed for Lough Foyle, to where the crippled *Donnell* was also towed. At NOB, Londonderry, the ship was found to be beyond economic repair for active service but she was used again – as a power generating source in the Normandy beachhead. *Donnell* lost almost thirty men dead. They were:

James R Beaumont, Jr
Eugene B Burdue
Harold Cohen
Guy R Coleman
John E Coppinger
William E Corzine
David W Danner
Lloyd A Dellinger
George E Ellison
Henry Ferrario
Robert E Fisher
Victor T Gallotto
Edgar L Guy
Robert C Hanrahan
James F Wright

James K Haworth
Landon Hendrix
Cortes D Jackson
William R Johnston
Richard H Johnston
Alonzo R Kashner, Jr
James H Mason
Thomas C Matelak
Edward L Moskal
Edward F Ryan
Arthur E Scheff
Thomas K Staton
Harry K Skyes
Frederick Wilklow

A more common experience for DE sailors was to lose ships from the convoys they were escorting. USS *Harveson* (DE-316), which had been in the same escort division as *Leopold* and *Joyce*, was on its second trip to Britain when, on 16

April 1944, just one day out of New York, SS *Pan Pennsylvania* was torpedoed. *Harveson* was ordered to continue with the convoy while *Joyce*, *Gandy* (DE-764) and *Peterson* (DE-152) hunted the submarine which was eventually forced to the surface; twelve submariners were taken prisoner. On the return trip to New York an aircraft covering the convoy picked up a submarine fifty miles behind; *Harveson*, *Peterson* and *Joyce* were detached to carry out a search which continued into the next day, 10 May, with the help of three Royal Navy vessels. Once again, however, the hunters drew a blank. Such experiences were typical of the service of submarine-hunting escorts: when a U-boat was detected long hours could be spent chasing it down. If the quarry was not destroyed there could be a feeling of frustration among crew members but they had still performed their role effectively: protecting convoys meant keeping U-boats away from merchant ships; a U-boat evading hunters in the deep could not threaten merchantmen. At this stage of the war U-boats were suffering heavy losses – a total of 242 would be lost during 1944 – and May 1944 saw only three Allied merchant ships sunk in the Atlantic with a total tonnage of 17,277. The second lowest tonnage of any month in the war to date, this had been bettered only by February 1944 when five ships totalling 16,628 tons had been lost.

The U-boat menace was far from over: in June 1944 over 80,000 tons of shipping, 22 vessels, went down in the Atlantic although such losses were well down on the days prior to May 1943 when the Allies had finally turned the tide of the Battle of the Atlantic.

The US Navy provided many escorts in 1942 and early 1943 but by the spring of 1943 only about two of every hundred escort vessels was from the US Navy. In March the Americans announced their intention to withdraw from North Atlantic convoy duties and the US Task Force based at Derry was accordingly disbanded on 1 June 1943. From that date the escort groups of the Royal Canadian Navy, previously under command of USN Task Group CGT. 24.7, came under the control of Commodore Simpson, the Royal Navy's Commodore (D), Western Approaches, at Derry. Simpson now had 'full and effective control over the operations, training and maintenance of all Escort Groups operating from or based at Londonderry, and also of those Groups of the Mid-Ocean Escort Force which use Londonderry as a turn-around base'. NOB, Londonderry began to be run down from mid-1943 and was finally disestablished on 15 August 1944, although the radio station remained in operation to provide the basis for a post-war US Naval Communications Station that did not close until 1977.

The Americans had put a large investment and much effort into their base and its facilities at Derry. For the most part, those facilities were happily shared with the Royal Navy and other Allied naval forces, although the original intention had been for Londonderry to be worked solely by the US Navy. There had, inevitably, been some areas of dissension: part of Beech Hill Barracks (Camp Holcomb) had been handed over to the Royal Navy for accommodation but when the British started adding improvements, in the form of an assembly hall, to the camp they ran into a dispute with US Navy authorities that ended in Royal Naval personnel moving from Beech Hill to Ebrington. Another dispute had arisen over ammunition storage in the area when the US authorities had declined to allow some British stocks to be held at Fincairn; an extension to

Kilnappy resolved this issue. And there were, of course, disputes between British and US servicemen that sometimes required considerable diplomacy to assuage.

No alliance can be free of friction and that is true of the Anglo-American alliance but it must be remembered that it was that Alliance that won the war and rarely was there a better expression on the ground of the special relationship than that between the Royal Navy and the US Navy in Derry.

In spite of their intentions the Americans did not withdraw completely from convoy escort tasks and US Navy ships could still be seen in the port, although their numbers were down and the frequency of visits much reduced. The main burden shifted to the Royal Navy and the Royal Canadian Navy on an almost-equal basis but, as the war moved into its final phase, the Canadians assumed the greater proportion. In the closing months of war US ships, operating under Admiralty control, would return to Londonderry and some would help to escort surrendered U-boats into Lisahally.

5

U-BOAT SIGHTED

One vital aspect of the Royal Navy's base that was kept secret throughout the war years, because of its importance to the battle of the Atlantic, was the Londonderry Anti-Submarine Training School which grew out of developments in the war against the U-boats and the need to co-ordinate those and further developments.

Early in the Battle of the Atlantic the Admiralty experimented with many devices and schemes intended to give the Royal Navy ascendancy over the enemy. Such experiments were not always successful. One unsuccessful idea was the creation of a combined striking force in March 1941 which may have owed something to a directive from Churchill himself. The striking force, under command of NOIC, Londonderry, was to include destroyers based at Londonderry and half the strength of the Coastal Command squadrons in Northern Ireland. The air element was to carry out sweeps every day over an extensive area north-west of Ireland. Should a sweep locate a U-boat then the surface striking force was to harry and hunt the submarine until it was destroyed; the ships were to carry on the hunt for forty-eight hours if necessary. Found to be of little effect, the experiment was abandoned. About all that could be said for it was that it provided some valuable experience, although it must also have produced considerable frustration. The Naval Staff History of the Second World War comments:

> The employment of destroyers in hunting groups for locating submarines was equally a mistake. A submarine which was . . . say, 60 miles away stood a very good chance of eluding the surface craft sent to look for her. The ocean is a wide area and the effective range of asdics is not more than 1,500 yards; if anti-submarine vessels take more than two hours to reach the reported position of the submarine, the one thing certain is that by the time they arrive at the spot the U-boat will be somewhere else. It is much the same as looking in a dark room for a black cat that isn't there. Convoy escorts are all too few, and to reduce them still further in order to provide hunting groups cannot be said to have been the best policy. This was the opinion of Vice-Admiral T H Binney's committee, which was then investigating war problems. They stated that 'the best position for anti-submarine vessels is in company with a convoy . . . For the present, every AS vessel with sufficiently good sea-keeping qualities should be employed with convoys rather than being dispersed in hunting groups',

A much more successful initiative was the establishment of the Londonderry Training School intended to give instruction in all aspects of anti-submarine warfare. This eventually grew into a combined services training centre.

The training role had actually begun at the end of 1940 with the stationing of a Royal Navy submarine in Lough Foyle to allow escort ships in the north-western approaches to practise submarine hunting. A second submarine was in use early in 1941 during the working-up programme for 'Town' class destroyers, the ancient American four-stackers given to Britain in exchange for bases in the western Atlantic and which Donald Macintyre described as 'vile little ships'. From such beginnings the anti-submarine school developed; the city remained the focal point of anti-submarine training, not only throughout the war but until 1970. By 1942 the school had become the principal training centre of its kind in the United Kingdom and made a lasting impression on US Navy personnel:

> The British 'dome-trainer', in which personnel were trained to the use of anti-aircraft guns in a sort of planetarium was of immense value to American gunners, as were the British 'tame submarines' on which escort vessels practised both day and night attacks. A destroyer's stay in port was so arranged that the last two days before sailing were given up to anti/submarine training. This system . . . sent sailors out on escort duty with a fresh knowledge of the actual sound and appearance of a submarine under various conditions.

In March 1942 a Western Approaches Training Unit (WATU) was established in Liverpool's Derby House, headquarters of Western Approaches Command, followed by the setting up of a similar unit in the Londonderry Anti-Submarine School in December. Both units consisted of a large room with the floor representing a stretch of mid-Atlantic ocean; across the floor members of the Women's Royal Naval Service, Wrens, moved symbols denoting U-boats, convoys and their escorts. Training officers 'commanded' the U-boats and tried to present the most difficult and aggressive tactical situations to the students, escort commanders, who were accommodated in small cubicles off the main room with vision restricted to what they could see through a slit in the wall; thus their view was similar to what they might have of the Atlantic from the bridge of a ship. Students were given reports of U-boat sightings or, in some cases, 'spotted' the boats themselves and then had to give orders to their escort force to hunt down and destroy the submarines. Through the use of WATU it was hoped that standards of operating might become consistent throughout all escort groups as it had been noted that some convoys suffered heavier losses than others in spite of having similar-sized escorts.

These were not the only innovations employed at the base. Since hunting and attacking U-boats at night was a particularly difficult and perilous task, the submarines being especially hard to counter in dark conditions, considerable attention was devoted to the problems of night attack. The Royal Canadian Navy had developed a 'night escort attack trainer' and a similar device was installed in a garage at the naval barracks, the first of its kind in the UK. The trainer further developed WATU's work by allowing accurate and realistic simulation of the hunt for and attack on a submarine at night from an escort's bridge. The training value of this innovation was 'the talk of those whose duties periodically carried them out north into Arctic waters or west across the Atlantic'.

Another function of the Londonderry base staff was gunnery training for ships from Liverpool and Greenock as well as from the Canadian and US Navies; this was conducted off Lough Foyle.

In January 1943 the new Commander-in-Chief, Western Approaches, Admiral Sir Max Horton, a former submariner, deciding that the work performed by the simulators needed a practical element, created a new element of the Londonderry Anti-Submarine School around HMS *Philante*, the luxury yacht donated to the Royal Navy by the millionaire industrialist and aviation pioneer T O M Sopwith. The yacht acted as a 'convoy' at sea while two British submarines, from Lough Foyle, played U-boats, and aircraft from the nearby airfields added the aerial dimension. Escort commanders were then able to practise bringing a 'convoy' safely through realistic attacks by the 'enemy'. Thus the work carried out earlier in the war, and that of the simulators, was combined most effectively.

Philante – the name derived from a combination of Sopwith's wife's name Phyllis and his initial 'T' – was commanded by the Training Captain (later Training Commander), Western Approaches. It was staffed by eleven specialist officers, including some Wrens, and operated from Larne as well as the Foyle in conjunction with its submarines and shore-based aircraft. One of its commanders, Evelyn Chavasse, described the commander's accommodation as a spacious sleeping cabin, a day cabin that would have aroused Nelson's jealousy, and a 'film star's bathroom'. An enormous polished mahogany dining table was complemented by cut-glass decanters and silver cutlery.

A further step occurred in April 1943 with the establishment of a Combined Service Anti-Submarine Training Centre to ensure the closest co-operation between escort vessels, Coastal Command aircraft, and aircraft of the Royal Navy's Fleet Air Arm. The Training Centre was based on the Foyle and the RAF fighter stations at Eglinton and Maydown were handed over to the Royal Navy, becoming HMS *Gannet* and HMS *Shrike* respectively on 15 May 1943.

The Foyle-based submarines also performed another training role: each time an escort group left the river to collect an eastbound convoy it would engage in simulated U-boat hunting with the submarines. The escort normally left port a day or two before taking over from the local escort. Evelyn Chavasse described how he would take his group 'with butterflies now fluttering wildly in my stomach' out of harbour to 'slip down the tortuous River Foyle from Londonderry to Moville and go out to sea to spend the intervening time on a strenuous programme of day and night exercises in the Irish Sea'. On the last day the group would fill up with fuel from the tanker at Moville, 'leave the last bags of mail in the tanker, and have a quiet night in bed' before a dawn rendezvous six miles west of Oversay.

As the war developed many other training facilities were created along the Foyle: these included an Operational Training Unit for Coastal Command crews at RAF Limavady, which included ASV (air-to-surface vessel radar) training, anti-Schnorkel training at the same base – from November 1944 – Coastal Command's Anti-U-boat Devices' School, also at Limavady and training for aircraft-carrier borne crews at Eglinton and Maydown. (See Chapter 6)

That training work was a major factor in the Battle of the Atlantic and enhanced escort crews' effectiveness. It also helped improve Coastal Command's effectiveness, and co-operation between airborne and seaborne anti-submarine hunters. In some respects lessons could have been absorbed more speedily since they had been there to study from the U-boat campaign of the First World

War. From such bizarre ideas (in 1914) as using a blacksmith's hammer to smash a submerged submarine's periscope before tying a bag around the periscope to blind the submarine and force it to surface, to trying to cordon off huge areas of water with nets and mine barrages, the Admiralty finally came round to the convoy system in 1917 with close escort provided by surface ships, flying-boats, which had earlier been used on search missions, and airships combining to defeat the U-boat. The clear lesson had been that close escort of convoys was vital: deploying significant numbers of ships or aircraft on hunting submarines on their transit routes was wasteful, since the advantage almost always lay with the U-boat. It was better to employ ships and aircraft in the vicinity of convoys, to which the U-boats must come to achieve their objective.

While the Admiralty quickly re-introduced the convoy system before the Second World War began, they believed that convoys with asdic-equipped escorts could defeat the U-boats; aircraft had no role other than to locate U-boats and direct ships to them. The strike force idea of 1941 not only was a formalisation of that thinking but demonstrated clearly just how long such thinking persisted. In 1941 the principle of meeting and beating the U-boats in the vicinity of the convoy had been finally and fully understood by the Admiralty and the number of escort groups was increased to provide concentration of escort forces. And, as Captain Donald Macintyre wrote in his book 'U-boat Killer'

> . . . maritime aircraft . . . might very well have 'turned the tide' long before May, 1943, had the principle been understood that the place to win the Battle of the Atlantic was in the vicinity of the convoys. So far as surface escorts were concerned this had been appreciated as far as back as 1941. . . (p109)

Much improved co-operation between maritime aircraft and surface vessels began to be the norm in early-1943 and had a chastening effect on the U-boats. With the addition of MAC-ships, merchant aircraft carriers converted from merchantmen, able to carry a flight of Swordfish biplanes, the German submariners began to be harried more and more. Horrendous U-boat losses led to Dönitz's order to withdraw the U-boats from the north Atlantic after May 1943. The co-ordination of escort vessels and land and sea-based aircraft is exemplified by the story of one escort group in May 1943. The group was C2 Escort Group, commanded by Lieutenant-Commander Evelyn H Chavasse, DSC, RN (later DSO), a native of West Cork. Although nominally Canadian, C2 was largely Royal Navy and considered itself part of the Londonderry Escort Force, although the Canadian authorities regarded it as being with the Newfoundland Escort Force. (To further confuse matters C2 was under operational control of the US Navy commodore in Londonderry while, in the eastern Atlantic it came under the strategic control of Commander-in-Chief, Western Approaches.) Evelyn Chavasse exercised command from the Town-class destroyer HMS *Broadway*, formerly USS *Hunt*, and the group also included HMS *Sherwood* (another Town-class), the British frigate *Lagan*, the Canadian ships *Drumheller*, *Morden* and *Chambly*, the British corvettes *Primrose* and *Snowdrop* and the French ship *Savorgnan de Brazza*. From time to time *Lagan* might be replaced by *Waveney*, and *Sherwood* by HMCS *St Croix*, while the corvette *Polyanthus* could also be under C2's command. Evelyn Chavasse took command of C2 in April 1942.

> From April 1942 to July 1943 . . . C2 Escort Group under my command escorted something like twenty convoys, mostly East and West across the North Atlantic, with an occasional switch to a Gibraltar convoy . . . Most . . . have now passed out of my memory, [as] I obediently did not keep a diary, and in my case most of the voyages were completely uneventful. It was my sad job to dodge U-boats, not to look for them; and with the help of intelligence from home, and our own skilful operators of radar and high-frequency direction-finding (H/F D/F)* on the spot, I became such an artful dodger that I was astonished to be told, on arrival at St John's, Newfoundland on a January day in 1943 that I had been awarded a DSC! I suppose I was given this for successfully running away from the enemy. . . .

While escorting convoy HX 237 to Britain in May 1943, C2, with air support, accounted for both U-89 and U-456. HX 237's passage is representative of how the battle turned against the U-boats and is also fairly typical of the operations of a Foyle-based escort group. The story of that convoy's passage, and of the destruction of the two U-boats, was told by Evelyn Chavasse in his unpublished book '*Business in Great Waters: war memories of a semi-sailor*'. Cancellation of North Russia convoys at this time had allowed Home Fleet destroyers to reinforce Atlantic convoy escorts as Support Groups, or in close escort.

> They were invaluable . . . Moreover, about this time the little Escort Carriers, with their ancient Swordfish aircraft, which flew so slowly that no German could believe it, so that their anti-aircraft fire almost invariably missed ahead, 'Woolworth Carriers' we called them [were introduced]. And finally the Coastal Command of the RAF, that Cinderella branch of the airforce, for years starved of aircraft in favour of Bomber and Fighter Commands, were suddenly remembered in Whitehall, and more and more very long range aircraft based at Home, in Iceland and the Azores, were able to cover the entire battle area. The U-boats didn't know what was coming to them.

C2 sailed from St John's on 6 May 1943 to rendezvous with the convoy and relieve the local escort. In his book on the Battle of the Atlantic, Donald Macintyre states that HX 237 lost three ships to U-boats but that three U-boats were destroyed. This does not tally with Evelyn Chavasse's memory which he was able to refresh from a post-war job in Admiralty Intelligence where a report on HX 237 showed that one or two ships of the convoy, not in the convoy, were lost, and five U-boats from a small pack of six were destroyed. Chavasse's own ship, *Broadway*, accounted for U-89, the 222nd U-boat to be sunk.

> If this particular convoy trip had a generally happy ending, it started from my point of view in annoyance, chaos and complete frustration. My Escort Group . . . was as usual short of several ships . . . and consisted of the *Broadway* herself, the only destroyer, the River class frigate, *Lagan* (Lieutenant-Commander Ayres), the British corvette *Primrose* (Lt Kitto), and the Canadian corvettes, my old faithfuls, *Morden*, *Drumheller* and *Chambly*. I also had a trawler *Vizalma* (Lt Angelbeck), and a tug. But, best of all, I was allotted for the first time a Woolworth Carrier equipped with Swordfish aircraft, HMS *Biter*, and three splendid Home Fleet destroyers, *Opportune*, *Obdurate* and *Pathfinder*.

* H/F D/F, or Huff Duff, enabled U-boats to be pinpointed by monitoring their radio transmissions from a number of known points.

At Argentia *Biter's* captain refused to position the carrier in the centre of the convoy where his destroyers would be able to 'reinforce the very sketchy close screen' and be available as a striking force. The carrier's captain insisted that he would operate, with his destroyers, between twenty to fifty miles from the convoy, which was following a very long southerly route, passing not far from the Azores.

> On 6 May, C2 Escort Group sailed from St John's, [although] the *Vizalma*, the tug and one merchant ship sailed late to intercept, and *Biter* and his boys sailed from Argentia. The usual thing happened, as so often in May: fog closed down. The convoy itself, unknown to me, became almost completely scattered and disorganised in the fog, and we had the greatest difficulty in finding it. Most of the Local Escort had lost touch, and the situation was most confused. Homing on to them by radar was useless, and we had to resort to a lot of chatter by R/T (radio/telephone) in an effort to make contact. No doubt U-boats were avidly listening and licking their chops in anticipation of finding a nice juicy convoy; and in fact I was rebuked from shore for using too much wireless. But there was no alternative. At dusk on the 6th we did find a few ships of the Western Local Escort . . . but no convoy, and throughout the night we chugged along together on convoy course and speed.
>
> As dawn broke, on the 7th, the weather was clearer. The *Biter*, who was to the northward of us, put up an air search, found the convoy, and signalled to me a course to steer, which turned out to be wildly wrong. I put all my ships on an extended screen at visual distance from each other and, by the greatest good fortune, the ship at the extreme end of the screen sighted the convoy on a totally different bearing. . . . By afternoon we were in touch.

However, two merchant ships never managed to find the convoy; one, or both, of these was torpedoed some days later while still searching for the convoy and its escort; these were the vessels which Macintyre wrongly described as being sunk while in convoy.

> The 8th May was still slightly misty. It was an uneventful day, as we six slow escorts got things organised into our own convoy routine, while the *Biter* . . . operated some 40 or 50 miles north of us. She sent out some air searches, but all her aircraft failed to find the convoy, and were therefore quite useless to me in detecting and reporting any U-boat which might be in a threatening position, because [the aircraft] didn't know our position.

With the relative positions of *Biter* and the convoy not clearly established the carrier was of no value either as a base for 'fixing' any high-frequency signals that might be intercepted from U-boats.

> On the following day, 9th May, the weather deteriorated, and the *Biter* was unable to fly off any aircraft. Visibility was low, there were many heavy rain squalls, and I took . . . *Broadway* into the centre of the convoy to fill up with fuel from a tanker. It was blowing quite hard, but all went well, and I took in a very useful amount of oil. But while we were still sucking greedily at the tanker, it started. The enemy had apparently mustered their forces, and were close on our heels. My memory of technical terms is now pretty shaky, but at that moment *Broadway* received what was called a 'close-range B-bar', in other words a wireless transmission from a U-boat, dead astern of the convoy, and not far away. We were temporarily connected by hosepipe to the tanker, and while we were hast-

> ily disengaging, I ordered *Primrose*, who was stationed astern of the convoy, to search and, if possible, attack. At the same time, I informed *Biter*, but she could not do anything useful, as she didn't know where we were. *Primrose*, however, actually spotted the U-boat, which hastily dived, but she did not make asdic contact and she later regained her station on the screen astern of the convoy.

At the Admiralty the folly of *Biter* operating so far from the convoy was recognised and her captain, who outranked Evelyn Chavasse, was ordered to take his ship and escorting destroyers into the convoy on 10 May; the convoy commodore made space for them in the middle. *Biter* and her destroyers were now to take orders from Chavasse.

> From that moment we never looked back, and she did magnificent work. *Biter* . . . became quite invaluable, and in spite of frequent foul weather, . . . and sometimes very foul weather, she never once refused a request of mine to fly off aircraft on a sortie. Her contribution consisted of a series of superb feats of sea-plus-airmanship in the most difficult conditions imaginable, and not a single aircraft was damaged. We were now a co-ordinated team with *Biter's* aircraft scouring the seas all around the convoy, *Biter's* destroyers, with their thirty knots plus, striking out . . . to put the fear of God into any U-boat the aircraft spotted and forcing it to dive and go blind, and my own little team, perhaps a little more experienced in these matters, providing the final close protection of the convoy.
>
> This change came none too soon. As soon as the *Biter* boys joined us, things began to happen thick and fast. *Primrose's* U-boat had evidently spread the news about us, and we had received a few more H/F D/F bearings of U-boat signals, but now they began probing in from various directions. It was clear to me that a wolf pack was forming, mainly to the north of us.
>
> On each occasion I asked *Biter* to send out a search in the most likely direction and also sent out one or two of her destroyers to back up the air search. In this way, several U-boats were sighted. For the most part, the U-boats stayed on the surface to fight it out with gunfire with the contemptible little Swordfish (one of our pilots was in fact wounded) but as soon as the destroyers came racing up at unprecedented speed, they dived in some haste. I don't think that any of the destroyers got in asdic contact with a submerged U-boat, but they probably kept them well down by plastering the area with depth charges. At least one can say that these tactics prevented the U-boats from concentrating, or even getting near the convoy, which at this stage was never closely threatened. The Admiralty stated that there were six U-boats trying to get at us, and as soon as we were within range, they sent shore-based aircraft . . . to operate under my direction. This enormously increased our field of vision around the convoy.

Night attacks were expected but did not develop; no night-flying was possible from *Biter*. At this time *Vizalma*, which had become separated from the escort group, suddenly re-appeared, being chased by a U-boat. A destroyer went to the trawler's assistance and the U-boat dived and escaped.

On 12 May, two days after the carrier had positioned herself in the centre of the convoy, a Liberator reported a U-boat. The aircraft had attacked and damaged the submarine which lay, stopped, on the surface some distance away off the convoy's port beam.

> This was too good to miss, and I sent off two of the destroyers to finish her off. This aircraft had not, however, previously contacted the convoy visually; and probably due to a navigational discrepancy and confusing reports of other U-

boats sighted in the same general area, the hunt was unsuccessful. The third destroyer was, as far as I can remember, sent out on a search astern, and so the convoy only had C2 Group with it. Thus came our chance. An aircraft from *Biter*, on her way back from a patrol and almost out of petrol, sighted a U-boat on the surface six miles ahead of the convoy. This was dangerous. I told the Commodore to turn the convoy ninety degrees to starboard, and as *Broadway* was the nearest and fastest of the Close Escort, I abandoned my position, and increased to 29 knots to attack, calling *Lagan* to follow me at her full speed of 20 knots. I handed over command of the escort to young Lieutenant Kitto in the *Primrose*, the senior corvette captain.

Meanwhile the aircraft had attacked with depth charges and possibly damaged the U-boat, which dived. There followed a piece of copy-book co-operation between us in *Broadway* and the aircraft. The latter dropped a smoke marker on the spot where the U-boat had dived, and flew back to the convoy. I told the pilot by radio/telephone which [was] my ship, and he circled and flew over me, waving cheerfully, and led me in a beeline to the smoke marker, which I duly sighted right ahead. Reducing speed I almost immediately got firm asdic contact, and the hunt was on. The convoy steamed steadily away from us, with little *Primrose* in charge. For once the weather was good.

Broadway made an attack, firing her depth charges from 'hedgehogs'. This first salvo missed. Then *Lagan* arrived, made contact by asdic and fired a pattern of depth charges which also missed.

There followed a prolonged hunt, and I still have a rather crumpled photocopy of the original plot of *Broadway's* movements: a most extraordinary document. U89 (I didn't of course know her number then!) had dived to a depth of about 400 feet. She was a wily bird, and . . . twisted and turned like a snake in ecstasy. *Lagan* and I shared the hunt, and between us we held her, and if one of us lost contact, the other regained it. Finally the lot happened to fall on *Broadway*. A salvo of bombs from our hedgehog soared beautifully into the air, . . . splashed in a neat circle 250 yards ahead of us, and then, after the usual anxious pause, we were at last rewarded with a lovely bang. We had hit her fair and square.

But I desperately wanted to make sure. I suppose I ought to have raced back to regain my place with the convoy and resumed command of the escort. But I didn't, and stayed where I was, sending *Lagan* back. (Her turn was to come later.) The reason I stayed was this. Time and time again, those of our escort vessels in other Groups with hedgehogs had made many *apparently* successful attacks on U-boats, and had been rewarded with a nice bang as one or more of the bombs had struck the U-boat's hull. *But there had never been any proof of a sinking*, and our confidence in this new weapon was beginning to waver, and morale in this respect was not high. I wanted *proof.*

So I continued my asdic sweep, and got a number of very woolly and indecisive echoes, which could possibly have been shoals of fish. Over an hour later, with the convoy now disappearing over the horizon, our patience was rewarded. For the first time in the war, a hedgehog produced tangible results (and when this was later made known, the morale of hedgehog-equipped ships rocketed). To my enormous relief, wreckage began to come up to the surface, and to the delight of my ship's company, we stopped and started picking up souvenirs . . . We didn't get much, but quite enough to satisfy ourselves: part of an electrical control panel with switches tallied in German, a rather dirty cotton singlet embroidered with an eagle and swastika, and a much-darned sock with the owner's name-tape in German . . . but without his foot inside. The crew of U89 were now lying in 1700 fathoms. May they rest in peace.

It didn't take us long to rejoin the convoy, and early next morning a Sunderland from home attacked another U-boat which had somehow managed to get uncomfortably close to the starboard side of the convoy. Perhaps it was the one which had so rudely chased the tug. *Drumheller*, who was nearest, closed the position, obtained asdic contact, and made a good depth-charge attack, which seems to have immobilised the U-boat (U456). *Lagan*, whom I had sent to help, strolled up and sank it. So easy. And produced more evidence.

And the battle was over. Just as we felt we were getting into our stride, *Biter* and her destroyers were withdrawn to assist another convoy in peril. Simultaneously, any survivors of 'our' wolf pack evidently decided to give it up as a bad job, and an unearthly silence descended over our stretch of the Atlantic, which for the past five days had been almost deafening with German and British radio. In defiance of King's Regulations and Admiralty Instructions, I exceeded my authority and ordered C2 Escort Group to Splice the Main Brace. A few days later, the convoy was delivered to England. On our arrival in Londonderry I received a telegram from the Admiralty that my father had died on 9th May.

By the end of the month, all U-boats had been temporarily withdrawn from the North Atlantic, and returned to their bases. For us, it was indeed a merry month of May. My father was, I am sure, very happy.

6

CONSTANT ENDEAVOUR

ALTHOUGH there were only 49 U-boats in May 1940, of which perhaps about a quarter were at sea at any time, their destruction rate was high: in May over 250,000 tons of shipping were sunk in the Atlantic by surface vessels, U-boats and aircraft; in June the figure topped 500,000, of which over half was attributable to U-boats, despite defective torpedoes (design faults in magnetic torpedo-firing pistols meant reverting to Great War vintage contact pistols until effective magnetic pistols were developed). Shipping losses for August totalled 56 merchantmen sunk by U-boats (over 260,000 tons) with another 15 (over 50,000 tons) sunk by aircraft. A shortage of escort vessels meant convoy escorts of as few as one or two ships; convoys of empty ships sailing to America could only be escorted 300 miles west of Ireland. Small wonder that U-boats were able to sink so many merchantmen – 73 escorted vessels and 144 unescorted vessels between July and October 1940 alone. This success against little effective opposition made this period of the war became retrospectively known as the 'happy time' to U-boat sailors.

By May 1941 there were 124 operational U-boats; the building programme increased the number to 236 on 1 December. Training crews and testing new boats, however, meant that the number entering operational service had not risen significantly until February 1941. Merchant shipping losses in the Atlantic reflected that increase: in March 1941 more than half a million tons were sunk; the next three months saw well over a million tons lost.

And Dönitz re-introduced the pack tactic in September 1940. The 'wolf pack' became a standard operational procedure: a group of U-boats, radio co-ordinated by U-boat Command from Kerneval, converged on their target at night, and on the surface, rendering asdic ineffective. Once a convoy was sighted, either by a U-boat, Luftwaffe aircraft, or intercept of British radio transmission, a pack would gather. Much depended on luck: a sighting by a U-boat was probably best since the boat could maintain station with the convoy keeping Kerneval appraised of its position. On 10 September, a pack of four U-boats attacked a convoy in a Force 8 gale, sinking five ships; just over a week later another convoy fell foul of a five-strong pack which sank eleven of fifteen ships and damaged a twelfth. October brought another series of wolf-pack successes: 38 ships from three convoys were lost over three consecutive nights.

Dönitz's new tactic caused the War Cabinet's Defence Committee to increase escort ship numbers by transferring vessels held in home waters for anti-invasion duties to trade protection. Among other measures taken to protect merchant shipping in the Atlantic had been the occupation of Iceland by British and Canadian troops in May 1940. The Danish colony had declared itself independent after Denmark was overrun; Iceland's location made it strategically important and the British-Canadian invasion was intended to pre-empt a similar German move. Iceland thereafter provided vital Atlantic naval and air bases for the Allies.

In August 1940 the Royal Navy received 50 obsolescent American destroyers from the US government in exchange for 99-year rent-free leases on British bases in the Bahamas, St Lucia, Jamaica, Trinidad and Antigua. These four-funnel destroyers, known as Town-class in the Royal Navy, were intended to alleviate the pressure on British escort ships. Town-class vessels worked up to operational readiness from Londonderry but their age and general unreliability made their crews feel that the Royal Navy had the worse side of the bargain although many gave sterling service despite their faults.

The U-boat 'happy time' was shortlived. In March 1941, when merchant shipping losses topped 500,000 tons, Royal Navy ships sank five U-boats, including three captained by some of Germany's most experienced commanders. Kriegsmarine submarine losses since the beginning of the war were now thirty-seven; thirty-eight boats were still operating while eighty-one were undergoing trials and training. A combination of factors was beginning to make life much more difficult for the U-boats.

As well as tactical improvements in Royal Naval operations, especially in the allocation of escort vessels, there were technical improvements in Coastal Command's aircraft, namely the fitting of an improved Air-to-Surface-Vessel radar, ASV II. The earlier ASV had required an aircraft to fly at 200 feet, a dangerously low level, to allow the operator to distinguish between a true 'contact' and 'clutter' caused by wave movements. ASV transmitted a series of pulses, the reflections of which were displayed on a screen: surface vessels appeared as blips along a central line and the operator could also see how far away the vessel was and whether it was left or right of the aircraft's line of flight.

Installed initially in Sunderlands, ASV II increased the likelihood of a surfaced U-boat being detected. Despite serviceability problems ASV II soon began to achieve results. U-boats had to surface for a time each day to recharge batteries and take in fresh air. ASV could direct an aircraft to a surfaced U-boat giving its crew the unpleasant experience of suddenly finding their boat being attacked by a plane carrying machine-guns and depth-charges. Until this time Coastal Command aircraft had not sunk any U-boats, although they had shared some 'kills' with escort ships and had damaged other boats; that was about to change.

Another technical breakthrough with significant long-term results was the British invention of a small 'resonant cavity magnetron' which allowed asdic's shortcomings to be overcome through a new centimetric shipboard radar capable of detecting surfaced U-boats at 4,000 to 5,000 yards; a skilled operator could even detect a submerged boat's periscope at up to 1,500 yards. In July 1941 the new radar was fitted to 25 corvettes; the number had doubled by December. Centimetric radar was later further refined for fitting to aircraft as ASV III.

In May 1941 U-100 was forced to surface after being depth-charged. The crew abandoned the boat, setting explosive charges to scuttle her. Those charges failed to explode and U-100 was boarded by British sailors who found the boat's codebooks and 'Enigma' encoding machine. Capturing this machine was a vital bonus in the war against the U-boats because the British 'Ultra' organisation at Bletchley Park was able to feed Naval Intelligence with copies of Kerneval's signals to the U-boats. This allowed the routing of convoys away from wolf packs, thereby reducing risk. Since the Germans were unaware of the capture of U-100's 'Enigma' machine, the Admiralty was careful not to make it too obvious that German naval signals were being read.

By the end of May 1941 U-boat operations in the Western Approaches had ceased with the submarines concentrating on central and southern Atlantic waters out of range of shore-based aircraft in Iceland, Northern Ireland and Britain.

Battles and campaigns have a habit of swinging back and forth and the U-boats now began to exact an appallingly high toll of merchant shipping in waters beyond air cover. During 1942 U-boats sank some 450,000 tons each month; although US shipyards were building dry-cargo ships faster than the loss rate, U-boats were sinking more tankers than were being built. As Correlli Barnett wrote, Dönitz was torpedoing his way to victory. On 24 October 1942, Winston Churchill wrote: 'There preys upon us as the greatest danger to the United Nations [the Allies], and particularly to our Island, the U-boat attack'. The U-boat menace was, Churchill later wrote, the thing that had scared him most during the war.

The USA's entry into the war had not brought an immediate diminution of the U-boat threat. Instead it had given the U-boats a second 'happy time', preying on unescorted merchant ships off America's east coast. Not until the United States instituted the convoy system in home waters was the German threat blunted there.

More resources than ever were deployed against the U-boats but those waging the struggle must often have wondered if the Germans were their only enemy. That was especially true for senior Coastal Command and Admiralty staff who found that the Air Council, the RAF's controlling body, and the Chief of the Air Staff were more concerned with the strategic bomber offensive against Germany than with giving Coastal Command sufficient aircraft to provide long-range cover for convoys.

Bomber Command's new chief, Air Marshal Sir Arthur Harris, convinced that he could bomb Germany into submission, refused to allow bombers to be diverted to Coastal Command, in spite of evidence that the U-boats would ground his bombers through lack of fuel long before those bombers could make a decisive impression on German industry. With some reluctance Bomber Command had, on Air Staff orders, loaned eight four-engined Liberators and four squadrons of twin-engined Wellingtons and Whitleys to Coastal Command in April 1942. In June the C-in-C, Home Fleet, Sir John Tovey, wrote that 'the Navy could no longer carry out its much increased task without adequate air cover; that support had not been forthcoming. The aircraft at the disposal of Coastal Command . . . were quite inadequate to meet their commitments'.

Portal, Chief of the Air Staff, suggested that the Admiralty was exaggerating the U-boat menace. A committee investigating the matter recommended temporarily transferring two Lancaster squadrons to Coastal Command; Portal rejected the recommendation. Harris enlisted Churchill on Bomber Command's side and the prime minister, in spite of his detailed knowledge of the U-boat threat, agreed to strengthen Bomber Command at Coastal's expense. Joubert, Coastal's chief, virtually in despair, noted that twenty-two new U-boats were being built every month whereas the destruction rate was only six or seven a month (September 1942). In October Churchill produced a document on 'Policy for the Conduct of the War', advocating yet again the primacy of Bomber Command. Although this was the paper in which he described 'the U-boat attack' as Britain's, and the Allies', greatest danger and acknowledged the Admiralty's call for greater air support, he proposed that 'for the present [we] try to obtain this extra effort from the United States' so as to encroach as little as possible on Bomber Command's operations.

Portal then presented a report estimating the effect of 4,000 to 6,000 British and American heavy bombers striking German targets in 1944. Pound, the First Sea Lord, countered with figures on the fuel needed for such operations showing that it would be impossible, at the current American tanker building rate, to bring in that fuel as well as the amounts already being imported. Pound then went to the Cabinet's new Anti-U-boat Committee and pressed the case for additional long-range aircraft to provide cover for convoys in 'the gap between the areas which can be protected by existing aircraft'. He estimated that 'at least 40 (with the necessary backing) are required, divided between Newfoundland, Iceland and Northern Ireland'. This pressure brought concessions but they were almost too little too late.

Clearly, Coastal Command had opponents even within the RAF: Portal still described it as 'defensive' in mid-1942. That Coastal Command played such an important part in the final victory is all the more creditable.

Coastal Command's bases in the north-west played a significant part in the war against the U-boat. The aircrews' work was generally unglamorous; long hours of patrols over the Atlantic's grey waters did not match the adventurous image of fighter and bomber crews. But those long, often boring, patrols helped beat the U-boats more effectively than Bomber Command's attacks on U-boat bases. In the Air Historical Branch's narrative 'T*he RAF in the Maritime War*' the contribution of the aircraft of Coastal Command is summed up:

> The immunity enjoyed by convoys when inside the range of full air cover was due, not to the lethality of air attack, but to the restriction it imposed on the free movement of surfaced U-boats watching for or following up on convoys. Although U-boats were being sighted and attacked by aircraft with increasing frequency, there was no corresponding increase in the numbers of U-boats destroyed or seriously damaged by these attacks. [Vol III, Atlantic and Home Waters p40]

This deterrent effect had forced the U-boats out of the Western Approaches, driving them to seek victims where no air cover was available. When very long range aircraft became available, nowhere was safe for the U-boats, for there were developments of ASV as well as aircraft-mounted searchlights (Leigh lights) that meant a surfaced submarine was not safe, even in darkness.

All that had yet to happen when Coastal Command began operating from Northern Ireland in September 1939. The Ansons of No.502 (Ulster) Squadron patrolling the north-western approaches could do little damage to any U-boats sighted, their only effect being to make them dive but, by January 1941, No.502 Squadron was at Limavady with Whitleys, including some fitted with the new ASV radar. Aircraft of A Flight had carried out the first ASV-equipped operation from Limavady in December 1940. ASV I was limited in its capabilities: the 200 feet height restriction to reduce surface 'clutter' limited effective range to three and a half miles. If contact was made at night, there was no effective method of illuminating the target for attack as the pre-war flares had not lived up to expectations. Not surprisingly it was November 1941 before a U-boat was sunk by an ASV-equipped aircraft.

No.502 Squadron was in action from Limavady on 10 February 1941 when Flying Officer (F/O) Walker attacked and badly damaged a U-boat some 300 miles off the north-west coast. During June F/O Holdsworth made two contacts in four days, attacking U-boats on both occasions. But the squadron lost a Whitley in July in air-to-air combat with a Focke-Wulf FW200 Condor. These four-engined bombers, converted from an airliner, were based in western France and Norway and could fly almost a thousand miles out into the Atlantic. They provided information on shipping movements for U-boat Command and attacked merchant shipping: in January and February 1941, Condors sank 46 ships (167,000 tons) against 60 sunk by U-boats.

In May 1941 No.502 Squadron deployed to St Eval in Cornwall to take part in the hunt for the German battleship, *Bismarck*. However, by the time 502 had reached St Eval the hunt for the *Bismarck* was all but over and the squadron returned to Limavady. In December that year a detachment went to St Eval to patrol U-boat transit routes in the Bay of Biscay and after Christmas the entire squadron transferred to Cornwall.

There had been other Coastal Command aircraft at Limavady. Hudsons from No.224 Squadron provided anti-submarine cover for convoys into and out of the Clyde and Mersey between April and December 1941. This squadron also moved to St Eval – its place at Limavady being taken by No.53 Squadron – but returned to the Foyleside in February 1942. Finally, in April 1942, 224 departed for Tiree.

Wellingtons, of 221 Squadron, had flown Atlantic patrols from Limavady between May and September 1941. They lost two aircraft in air combat but attacked four U-boats and carried out 92 operational sorties in July. No.221 left Limavady for Iceland but put in a short re-appearance at Aghanloo in December prior to moving to the Middle East.

In April 1942 Limavady began a two-year period without operational flying, becoming home to No.7 Operational Training Unit (OTU) which formed there on 1 April 1942 to carry out maritime reconnaissance and ASV training with Wellingtons and Ansons.

The OTU's overwater flights led to a number of accidents for which Limavady was notorious; the proximity of Benevenagh made for some hair-raising moments, especially in poor visibility, and the mountain became known as 'Ben Twitch'. On one unfortunate night in January 1943 three aircraft were lost from 7 OTU: one struck Benevenagh; another crashed near Ballykelly; and the third went into Lough Foyle where it was found on the morning of the 3rd.

In January 1944 the OTU left and No.612 Squadron, Coastal Command, arrived with Wellingtons. These were Wellington XIVs fitted with ASV and Leigh

Lights, which allowed an attacking aircraft to illuminate its target in the dark. The Leigh Light had been developed by Squadron-Leader H de V Leigh by fitting a 24-inch naval searchlight into the belly of an ASV-equipped Wellington. Trials showed considerable promise: indeed, having detected a surfaced British submarine with ASV, the trials aircraft was able to switch on the Leigh Light and illuminate the sub before the crew even heard the Wellington's engines. The 'attack' lasted for 27 seconds, thus proving that the light would allow an aircraft an advantage in the 25 seconds between being spotted by a U-boat's lookouts and the boat's submerging. Those trials took place in May 1941 but more than a year passed before the Leigh Light was operational, due to initial opposition by Air Marshal Sir Philip Joubert de la Ferté, the new chief of Coastal Command, and difficulties in fitting equipment to operational aircraft. The Leigh Light proved a most useful piece of equipment and, in the hands of crews of No.612 and other squadrons, helped bring about the demise of many U-boats.

However, 612's first U-boat 'kill' from Limavady was achieved without the use of the Wellington's Leigh Light when Pilot Officer (P/O) Paynter's machine picked up the surfaced U-545 on ASV on 10 February 1944. Paynter was able to attack without his Leigh Light as conditions were good, although it was ten minutes before midnight.

> The crew reported a perfect straddle and the contact disappeared 2 minutes after the attack. Debris, oval objects and small orange lights appeared on the surface 7 minutes later. At 0310 hours, Wellington '0' [Paynter's aircraft] landed at base.

U-545's crew were rescued by another U-boat. That same night Warrant Officer Ward of 612 Squadron, flying a Wellington borrowed from No.407, also based at Limavady, obtained an ASV contact which was then lost. At 0235 hours there was a further contact and Ward attacked a U-boat using his Leigh Light although a 'kill' was not claimed. Another aircraft, flown by F/O Heron of 407, had a contact that night.

> a radar contact was obtained dead ahead at 6 miles. At three eighths of a mile the Leigh Light was switched on, illuminating a U-boat on the surface . . . The aircraft attacked immediately, crossing the U-boat just forward of the conning tower. 6 Mark II depth charges were dropped from 60 feet, set for depth 25 feet. Explosions were seen around the U-boat. After this the U-boat opened fire on the aircraft. The aircraft crew reported a dull glow from the U-boat as if she was on fire but no conclusion could be drawn.

U-283 went down with no survivors. Eight days later 407 Squadron had an 'almost certain' kill when F/O Hyslop's aircraft attacked a submarine but the squadron's time at Limavady was drawing to a close as was that of 612. The latter left Limavady on 6 March while the former departed on 28 April. Limavady, for a time, had no Coastal Command units, playing host instead to a series of Fleet Air Arm squadrons.

Coastal Command returned with Leigh Light Wellingtons of Nos 172 and 612 Squadrons at the beginning of September. The Operations Record Book (ORB) of the latter summarised the situation at Limavady.

> A number of U-boats have been attacking and sinking our shipping in the Western Approaches and the Navy, although it has large escort groups in the area,

> has not yet had any concrete success against them. Consequently, a number of anti-submarine squadrons of Coastal Command have been moved to No.15 Group area. It appears that the squadron will once more revert to its original role of flying only by night. . . . The areas . . . in which the patrols are being flown are both small and entirely localised; rarely do they take our crews more than 100 miles from base.

The U-boats had developed a new system of taking in fresh air and recharging their batteries while submerged by using a breathing pipe, or Schnorkel, extending from the boat to the surface; Schnorkel-equipped boats could remain underwater for several days. Although an intensive anti-Schnorkel training programme was begun in November there were no successes resulting from radar detections of the tiny Schnorkel devices.

In mid-December 1944, No.612 departed Limavady for the last time while No.172 remained to carry out Atlantic patrols until the war ended; the squadron disbanded in June. Coastal Command had also set up an Anti-U-boat Devices School at Limavady which closed, after four months, following VJ Day in August and brought the life of RAF Limavady to an end.

The end of the war did not spell the end of the other Coastal station near Limavady. RAF Ballykelly was to survive as a coastal base for another quarter of a century after wartime service as one of Coastal Command's most important bases.

The first Command unit to arrive was Coastal Command Development Unit (CCDU) at the beginning of December 1941. Equipped with various aircraft types, including Beauforts, Hudsons and Whitleys, CCDU moved to Scotland in June 1942 to allow No.220 Squadron's Boeing Fortresses to move in; initially there were only two of the American heavies.

The four-engined Fortresses were engaged on largely uneventful convoy escort patrols. Eleven new Fortress IIs arrived in July and, by the month's end, most had flown operationally. A similar pattern of operations, mostly anti-submarine sweeps and convoy escorts, was carried out in August which

> was marred by disaster on the 10th, when two Fortresses were lost, chiefly because of bad weather. In one case, Fortress 'N' crashed near Acklington, while returning from convoy escort, although the crew all baled out and landed safely. In the second incident, Fortress 'J', while returning from convoy escort in very bad weather, crashed near Nutts Corner, killing all on board. They were Warrant Officer Sanderson, Flight Sergeant (F/Sgt) Bristowe, F/Sgt Capel, Sgt Garcia, Sgt Fretter and Sgt Foster. The aircraft had taken off at 1946 hours and crashed at 2330 hours, exploding the depth charges.

The squadron also flew air-sea rescue missions: on 27 September a Fortress spotted a lifeboat and rafts, with about fifty men, close by a large amount of floating wreckage and debris. Smoke and flame floats were dropped, as well as rations, and the aircraft gave directions to the lifeboat to guide it to the rafts.

Early in 1943 No.220 had two successes against U-boats. On the morning of 3 February P/O Ramsden sighted a U-boat, some 29 miles from a convoy.

> The U-boat was sighted from 3000 feet . . . [and] was attacked . . . from a height of 50 feet, with 7 torpex filled 250lb depth charges. The centre of the stick was estimated to be from 10-20 feet ahead of track. A purple patch of oil was seen in

> the centre of a patch of disturbed water immediately after the attack but this quickly dispersed in the rough water. After 20 minutes, smoke floats and sea markers were dropped at 6-mile intervals from the scene of the attack to the convoy. . . .

The destruction of U-265 was later confirmed. The second boat to fall prey to 220 was U-624 which was sunk on 7 February by P/O Roberson's crew.

> While on convoy escort . . . Fortress FL459 'J' sighted a U-boat on the surface. After stalking through cloud cover to within 3 miles, the aircraft attacked through rain at 90 degrees to track from starboard, with depth charges. The U-boat was straddled between numbers 4 and 5 depth charges and then submerged very slowly. After the plume subsided, a round object 12 feet long rose out of the water to about 4 feet and several pieces of yellow wood were also seen.

No.220 Squadron left Ballykelly for Aldergrove on 14 February. Also at Ballykelly by this time was No.120 Squadron, destined to be Coastal Command's most successful unit in the U-boat war. No.120 had moved in on 21 July 1942 from Nutts Corner with four-engined Consolidated Liberators; the squadron's aircraft had already used Ballykelly occasionally.

The Liberators were the longest-legged aircraft in the RAF's inventory and played a vital part in providing air cover to Atlantic convoys. It is all the more surprising that 120, formed specially to operate the Liberator, had never more than nine aircraft at any one time in the two years from September 1941.

On 16 August 1942 Squadron Leader (S/Ldr) Terence Bulloch, a Lisburn man who was to become Coastal Command's highest-scoring 'ace', made contact with a convoy of 33 ships, escorted by three sloops, two corvettes and an RAF Lancaster bomber. At 1935 hours, Bulloch attacked a U-boat, dropping six depth charges as it dived. Although 'the conning tower lifted out of the water, wreckage was seen afterwards and 3 sea markers were dropped' the attack was not confirmed as a 'kill'.

Bulloch went with a detachment to Reykjavik from early September. While flying from Iceland, he scattered a wolf pack that threatened convoy HX 217 which had already suffered seven attacks. A submarine was attacked and sunk at 0929 on 8 December. Just over three hours later two surfaced U-boats were spotted; Bulloch attacked one and the other dived. Less than two hours afterwards, another U-boat was attacked with cannon-fire, Bulloch having dropped all his depth charges. A further cannon attack was made on another boat twenty-three minutes later, followed by three more attacks on different boats. During the last attack the aircraft's cannons jammed but the rear gunner fired 100 rounds into the conning tower. During this patrol Bulloch had sunk two U-boats, although one was not confirmed, and forced six others to dive, ending their threat to the convoy. The patrol exemplified the value of long-range air cover.

When 120 moved to Aldergrove on 14 February 1943, Ballykelly was left without operational aircraft. As with Limavady the Royal Navy disembarked Fleet Air Arm squadrons there but Coastal Command returned with No.86 Squadron, flying Liberators, from 3 September until March 1944 when they moved to Iceland from whence 120 returned to Ballykelly. Almost as soon as the squadron was back, it was in action. Flight Lieutenant (F/Lt) Kerrigan attacked a U-boat which stayed on the surface, as was now increasingly the case, to fight it out. One of Kerrigan's crew was killed and his plane lost an engine despite which he attacked two more submarines; two more crew members were fatally wounded and another engine knocked out.

The squadron was kept busy with patrols until the war ended: in July 1944 a total of 61 sorties was flown; August saw 67 and the total for September was up to 89. In September the squadron co-operated closely with escort groups in the North Channel and north-north-west of Ireland while 'the Navy's order to fishing vessels not to operate East of 10 degrees W was a great boon to us as, prior to this, aircraft were continually homing on to and then illuminating [with Leigh Lights] fishing vessels'.

From then until May 1945 over 500 sorties were flown with as many as eight missions a day in March 1945; there were some sightings and attacks but no confirmed 'kills'. Nonetheless, No.120 Squadron ended the war as Coastal Command's most successful squadron with 16 confirmed 'kills'. Although the squadron disbanded on 4 June 1945 it subsequently reformed and is still in the RAF's order of battle fifty years later.

The final Coastal squadron to operate from Ballykelly was No.59 Squadron, also Liberator-equipped, which arrived in September 1943. Many patrols were flown but submarine sightings were relatively few, although there was one by a Ballykelly-based aircraft on 16 October and some 59 Squadron machines based on Iceland also made attacks. However, there were air combats with Luftwaffe planes: an inconclusive battle between F/Lt Teare's FL977'H' and a FW200 in September 1943 was followed by a brush between the same pilot and a Blohm und Voss BV222 on 22 November.

The routine for 1944 was much the same, broken by some air combats and attacks on U-boats which resulted in probable 'kills'. During November 1944 50 sorties were flown, of which seventeen were convoy escorts.

> A feature of the month's activities was the close to the coast escorting of convoys when there was reason to believe a U-boat might be patrolling. During the 17 convoy escorts flown during the month no ships were lost and this was deemed a success for the squadron.

January 1945 started quietly but in the second week U-boats sank three ships in as many days and the squadron's sortie rate increased to five per day, although this was also to compensate for one of No.120's flights being stood down to convert to Liberator VIIIs. A total of 76 sorties was flown during the month. In February there were 96 missions with some attacks on Schnorkels with no apparent results. In spite of beginning conversion to Liberator VIIIs with their much superior ASV XA the squadron still flew 68 operations. Crews were pleased with the new radar which they 'considered to be a brilliant instrument of detection' in the closing weeks of war.

In the autumn of 1945 the squadron moved to Cambridgeshire where it was disbanded. Ballykelly's aircraft had played a vital part in the Battle of the Atlantic and the airfield itself, with two 2,000-yard runways, was an ideal base for the Liberators which did so much to bring about the defeat of the U-boats.

Just up the road from Ballykelly was another airfield at Eglinton, still in use today as a civil airport, while closer to the city was yet another field at Maydown, today an industrial complex. Both had been fighter airfields, although originally intended for Coastal Command, but were handed over to the Admiralty in 1943 for Fleet Air Arm use. On 15 May 1943 Eglinton was commissioned as HMS *Gannet* and Maydown as HMS *Shrike*. Both had important, if unspectacular, roles to play in the final phase of the Battle of the Atlantic.

Eglinton provided a base for forming and training Fleet Air Arm fighter squadrons. To support this function 725 Naval Air Squadron formed on 27 August for target towing and other duties associated with fighter pilot training. Equipped with Blackburn Rocs, Blackburn Skuas and Miles Martinets, the squadron remained at Eglinton until September 1945. Among fighter units which formed at HMS *Gannet* were 1835 and 1837 with Chance-Vought Corsairs; shortly after VE Day, 891 and 892 squadrons formed on Grumman Hellcats. After the war *Gannet* remained in commission and provided a centre for naval aviation training until its closure in 1959. Ironically, among the last units to form and train at Eglinton in 1958 was an anti-submarine squadron of Fairey Gannets for the new Federal German Navy's air arm, the Marineflieger.

Maydown, or HMS *Shrike*, had a shorter life than Eglinton but, at the end of the war in Europe, it was home to the Royal Navy's largest single squadron, 836 with Fairey Swordfish. No.836 moved into Maydown in June 1943 on a temporary basis as the airfield, with Eglinton, was due to be handed over to the Americans in October 1944. This latter plan never materialised and Maydown carried on performing a very important task for the Atlantic convoys with 836 Squadron's Swordfish, the slow, flimsy, ancient biplanes that flew from MAC-ships to provide air cover across the entire Atlantic.

Soon after arriving at Maydown the squadron absorbed Nos 838 and 840 Squadrons, No.700W Flight and detachments of Nos 833 and 834 Squadrons to bring its strength up to 27 Swordfish and two Supermarine Walruses; the latter pair were soon given up. Training was carried out by 744 Squadron which later converted to Fairey Barracudas for anti-submarine training.

The Swordfish of 836 Squadron formed a pool from which MAC-ship flights were formed. As the MAC-ship building programme progressed additional flights formed at Maydown until, eventually, the station had almost 100 aircraft. 836's deployed in 23 three, or four, aircraft flights, designated 836A Flight to 836Z Flight; no flights were designated I, O or S.

The work of the Swordfish of No.836 Squadron is well illustrated by Evelyn Chavasse's account of HMS *Biter's* support of his escort group in May 1943. As well as 836, a second Swordfish 'pool' squadron providing flights for the MAC-ships took up residence at Maydown in December 1943. This was No.860 Squadron whose crews were mainly Dutchmen of the Royal Netherlands Navy; with 836 the Dutch squadron formed the MAC-ship Wing. Aircraft of 860 deployed as O and S Flights aboard MV *Acavus* and MV *Gadila* respectively; O Flight transferred to MV *Macoma* in June 1944 and was later redesignated F Flight after 836F Flight was disbanded.

The venerable Swordfish did sterling work aboard the MAC-ships. Although obsolete when war began, the Swordfish outlived its successor, the Albacore, in front-line service. As convoys handed over to the local escort force off the north coast the Swordfish would leave their carriers and fly into Maydown, returning to provide cover as another convoy left home waters for North America. The sight, and sound, of these ancient biplanes was a comfort to the merchant seamen as their vessels plodded through the ocean: the crewmen knew that the aircraft were an invaluable deterrent to U-boats.

Eglinton and Maydown also saw much training work in co-operation with escorts (see Chapter 5) and, in this role, helped seal the final fate of the U-boat service. Maydown closed in September 1945, although it re-opened for a short time as HMS *Gannet II* before closing finally in January 1949. The squadrons of the MAC-ship Wing disbanded on 21 May 1945 (836) and 1 August 1945 (860) having performed extremely important and arduous, if unglamorous, service in the Battle of the Atlantic.

The airfields of the north-west were a strategic asset in the U-boat war and, as co-operation between air and surface escorts improved, took an increasing part in the defeat of the German submarines. Their work, especially that of the Coastal Command bases at Limavady and Ballykelly, was helped by the fact that the Irish government permitted aircraft from the north-west to fly over Donegal on their way out to Atlantic, thus reducing flying distances and adding to the time that could be spent on patrol.

7

ON THE HOME FRONT

War brought a kaleidoscope of experiences to residents of the city. There was the initial rush to institute civil defence procedures and the implementation of rationing, although the latter never affected Derry quite as much as it did other areas of Northern Ireland and Britain itself. Then there was the upsurge in the service population of the city: from an infantry battalion of about 1,000 men in 1939 the local service population grew to a peak, in 1943, of well over 30,000 and, if the airfields at Maydown, Eglinton and Ballykelly are added in that figure would come closer to 40,000.

The creation of the Londonderry naval base meant re-opening the old Derry shipyard, development and expansion at that yard and, for only the second time in the city's modern history, full employment – this too in 1943. Into the shipyard came a branch of the Belfast shipbuilders, Harland and Wolff, at Strand Road while two local companies, Browne's and Craig's, received Admiralty contracts to carry out repair work on ships.

The addition of an American element at the yard brought even more activity. Much of the work was routine, but important nonetheless. And there were times when it was far from routine. Damage to ships by enemy action, or severe weather, called for extensive repairs. On occasion the experiences of workers on badly-damaged ships could be horrendous. Normally, when there had been loss of life, apprentices were not allowed into the affected areas but this did not always happen. Vance Crockett, a Harland and Wolff apprentice, remembered one ship with damage from an explosion, either a mine or a torpedo strike. Steel plates were curled over on themselves 'like a swiss roll', a common sight on a damaged vessel. Young Crockett saw what he assumed to be a lump of seaweed sticking to a length of curled plate. Reaching out to remove it, he discovered it was a human scalp, the grisly remains of a sailor who had perished in the explosion that had rocked his ship.

In February 1943 the Grimsby-class sloop HMS *Londonderry* was towed into her name port with extensive damage to her stern. The official record notes the cause of the damage as an underwater explosion but it was generally believed that *Londonderry* had been hit by an acoustic torpedo, a new German weapon that homed onto the sound of a ship's propellers. *Londonderry* was probably the first victim of this weapon. The shipyard made temporary repairs which allowed the sloop to leave under her own steam for further repairs in Britain; some months later HMS *Londonderry* was back in action escorting convoys.

The acoustic torpedo required a countermeasure and the brains of the Admiralty's backroom teams were applied to the problem. Their solution was first put into action in Derry's dry dock. Vance Crockett recalls an escort ship being docked to have a cage structure fitted around its propeller, the trailing edges of which were drilled out with a series of holes. A compressor was also fitted to the vessel to blow air into the structure. Few understood the purpose of the work which was supervised by a female scientist believed to have been from the Admiralty but the ship later went to sea to try out the newly-installed equipment, which was an early anti-cavitation device designed to cut propeller noise and reduce the risk from acoustic torpedoes. The trials proved successful and the anti-cavitation device was later fitted to other ships. Such devices are now built in to warships at the construction stage, the compressed air being passed through the hollow propeller shaft.

There was nothing glamorous in the work of the city's shipyard, yet it was vital to the war effort and the U-boats' eventual defeat. A similar comment could also be made about the city's shirt factories which, in the course of the war, produced the largest proportion of the British Army's shirts. Those included a special heavy double-fronted shirt for winter wear which was particularly appreciated by soldiers suffering through the cold winter of 1944/45 in North-West Europe, on the Italian front, or in Britain on freezing AA gunsites where such shirts were worn by men of 9th (Londonderry) HAA Regiment, some of whom had worked in the very factories that produced their shirts. Other items of uniform were also made in Derry as were shirts for the other services; the Canadian forces received numbers of Derry-made shirts although the bulk of production went to British soldiers.

The immediacy of war was never far away from those involved in work related to the war effort while the presence of so many servicemen of various nationalities was a constant visual reminder of the war in the streets of the city. So too was the blackout and the other civil defence precautions in operation. Around the city were a large number of Morrison shelters, intended to provide protection in the event of bombing raids. The city centre had the largest concentration of these, usually, red-brick constructions and the last was only demolished in recent years when the former Richmond factory at Strand Road became a supermarket. In the Diamond two shelters were built and connected to an underground civil defence control centre.

As well as Air Raid Protection (ARP) Wardens who ensured that blackout regulations were enforced, as well as being available for emergency services, there was a fire-watching service provided by employees of local companies who would spend nights on the premises ready to take immediate action in the event of firebombing. The fire service provided training courses for individuals on dealing with incendiary bombs; these were organised at several venues, including Brooke Park.

Many local people had relatives in the forces and were anxious to know what was happening on the various fronts. Some became involved in schemes to raise funds for comforts for servicemen, either those based in the city or the city's own sons serving in 9th (Londonderry) HAA Regiment. The owner of the All Cash Stores, Mr Porter, led efforts to provide comfort funds for the local batteries of 9th Regiment; the balance of those funds held by 24 and 25 HAA Batteries later built the Services Club in Crawford Square.

But the most poignant reminder of the war for many families was the telegram from the Admiralty, War Office, or Air Ministry telling that a loved one had been killed in action, or wounded, or taken prisoner. More than 200 local homes received such telegrams.

There were other deaths as a result of the war. Those killed in the one air raid on the city were a reminder of what the toll might have been had the Luftwaffe come back in force to the west in the winter of 1941/42. Determined attacks on Derry would have left the city devastated, with a massive civilian death toll far in excess of the city's service death toll and the face of the city would have been changed beyond recognition. That Derry was spared is due to Hitler's decision to attack the Soviet Union and to the fact that that attack was delayed by British intervention in Greece in early 1941, an episode of the war in which a number of Derrymen, volunteers from 9th Regiment, who had transferred to 20 HAA Battery, were captured by the Germans.

Air raid precautions created their own hazards. The blackout caused many deaths throughout the UK, resulting in blackout regulations being relaxed slightly. Air raid shelters had corners painted white, bands of white were applied to such hazards as lamp-posts, pillar boxes and even trees, while steps at Lower Fountain Hill were painted with a pattern of black and white to help those negotiating them in darkness; similar patterns were painted on kerbs elsewhere. But there was still the problem of almost complete darkness, especially on nights when there was no moonlight. On one such night a young cyclist died when his bicycle collided with a car at Prehen and many serious injuries resulted from people running, or walking, into unseen obstructions. Pedestrians were permitted to carry a small torch as long as the light was obscured by two layers of tissue paper and the torch was pointed downwards. Those out at night were urged to 'wear something white'.

Dark nights brought fear to many. A common image of the war years is of the social sparkle of dances in the halls around the city. But there was also a down side to this. The author's mother, who lived in Rosemount, told of leaving a dance in the Guildhall at quarter to eleven one night, in order to be home, as she was required to be, by eleven o'clock. As she made her way up William Street in total darkness she could hear another set of footsteps, those of a male, behind her and gaining on her. Near the top of William Street was a Morrison shelter and she decided to do what she would never otherwise have contemplated doing: she removed her shoes and stepped between the shelter and the wall. The baffled pursuer ran around the shelter and into Francis Street. When the sound of his footsteps had receded she came out of hiding and, carrying her shoes, ran up Creggan Street and Creggan Hill, not stopping until she reached her own home. Such an experience was not unusual and many women who lived through the war could tell of something similar.

The blackout also brought a considerable shock one evening to two middle-aged spinster sisters. Devout Catholics who attended Mass daily, the two ladies were sitting in the back room of their home when the door burst open and a group of inebriated Canadian sailors entered. The Canadians had been passing the end of the street when they had noticed the glow of the lamp in front of the sisters' image of the Sacred Heart and had mistaken the red glow for something completely different; the two women had forgotten to pull the blackout blind in their front room that evening. The Canadians may have been among the customers of several local individuals who were convicted of running 'disorderly houses'; local newspapers record three such convictions in 1943 alone.

Another by-product of the blackout was an increase in burglaries, with shopkeepers being especially concerned about the incidence of theft. The blackout was a thieves' charter as criminals could avoid detection quite easily. Towards the end of the war that charter ran out as restrictions were eased and then virtually eliminated.

On one wall in Foyle Road can still be seen a faded yellow sign indicating the direction to a First Aid Post. Many such posts were located around the city with local doctors providing the service. One young GP, Austin Kinsella, a native of Dublin, who had been appointed as a Medical Officer to the RAF in the city, and who was also responsible for the First Aid Post at Gwynn's Institute in Brooke Park, thought that he might be able to obtain an additional fuel ration for his motorcycle by suggesting to the authorities that he could raise and train a First-Aid motorcycle flying squad. He was amazed at the response: rather than additional fuel coupons he was given a number of motorcycles and as much fuel as he needed. The flying squad was soon fully staffed with no shortage of volunteers wanting to join.

Co-located with many First Aid Posts were Gas Cleansing Stations intended to decontaminate anyone caught in the open in a gas attack. The advice given was that if clothing had been splashed by liquid gas the victim should immediately remove all outer garments and go as quickly as possible to the nearest house, Gas Cleansing Station, or Mobile Gas Cleansing Unit and wash his or her body thoroughly with plenty of soap and water. Before the war it had been feared that extensive use might be made of gas; as a result, arrangements were made for everyone to have a gas mask, which was to be kept close at hand in case of gas attack. Special infant masks were also provided for babies; these cocooned the child completely and were fitted with a foot pump to fill the container with oxygen. Leaflets on gasproofing rooms in private houses were issued together with information on identifying gases by smell while the tops of pillar boxes were treated with a chemical paint that would change colour if gas was present.

Gas masks are one of the most persistent memories of the war along with the blackout and rationing. The latter was introduced in September 1939 for petrol and led to restricted bus services in the city as the Northern Ireland Road Transport Board decided to stop the buses at 7pm each evening. On 8 January 1940 rationing was applied to butter, margarine, sugar, cooking fats and meat. As the war progressed rationing was extended, with commodities such as tea added to the list, while the ration scale of many products varied, usually downwards, at times. Obtaining rationed foodstuffs from Éire was an offence punishable by six months' imprisonment, unless it was sent as small gifts. The jail sentence did not act as a deterrent to many: soldiers of 2nd/7th Warwicks found, soon after arriving in Ebrington Barracks, that they could obtain good supplies of fresh meat and many took the opportunity to send parcels of meat home to their families.

Rationing gave rise to increased smuggling. When clothing was added to the list of rationed items it provided further incentive for cross-border trips. Smugglers often resorted to wearing old garments on the outward bound journey and the replacements on the return trip. Patrols of B-Specials in border areas assumed the duties of customs officials and often confiscated smuggled goods. There was a general feeling that such confiscated goods found their way into the homes of members of the patrols. Furniture was another addition to the rationing scheme as thousands of families throughout the UK were bombed out of their homes. In order to make replacement furniture available to such families, and to newly-weds, furniture purchase was restricted by rationing and the introduction of the 'Utility-mark' scheme. This mark, like two cheeses each with a segment removed, was applied to an approved range of furniture but could also be found on clothing and lasted into the 1950s. Even buses were constructed to a 'Utility' standard in order to conserve materials.

Wartime memories of the city are vivid for those who lived through the period: they are memories of sights, like the many uniforms of the various servicemen in the area; and sounds, like the wailing of the wind in the rigging of barrage balloons; and smells, like the rubber of the gasmasks that were everywhere. Many even remember the taste of bananas but it was only taste: no bananas were imported into the UK during the war and, as a substitute, mashed boiled parsnips had banana flavouring added.

But there were other memories, like the visits to the city of personalities such as Mrs Eleanor Roosevelt, or Lord Louis Mountbatten while some Derry, and Donegal, people recall meeting Mountbatten's nephew, Philip, the future Duke of Edinburgh, as a young naval officer. And, following the end of war in Europe, King George VI and Queen Elizabeth visited the city; among the soldiers lining the streets on that occasion was a party from 9th (Londonderry) HAA Regiment, brought over specially from their base in England.

Most of those who visited the city in the war years did so almost anonymously, like the Gibraltarian refugees who came to Northern Ireland in 1944 after V1s started landing in England; groups were accommodated in Derry at Ballougry and near Lisahally. Those same V1s that prompted the evacuation of the Gibraltarians also took the lives, in January 1945, of two young Derrymen who had been sent by the labour exchange to work in England.

Close by the second group of refugees was a prisoner-of-war camp. Not all the prisoners were U-boat sailors; some were soldiers or airmen, among them a German paratrooper later to become famous as Manchester City's goalkeeper, Bert Trautmann. Some prisoners were only in the city for a very brief time, like the two Italian submarine officers who were landed at Derry on 26 July 1942. The pair, survivors of an Italian sub sunk off the Azores, were handed over to the Military Police who escorted them to London.

Perhaps the Italian prisoners did not have time to form an opinion about Derry but other visitors, from the Allied forces, did. Many still have fond memories of the city on the Foyle that welcomed them after long Atlantic voyages, or that was home while they manned AA guns or barrage balloons or kept aircraft flying.

Edward C McCudden served in C Battery of the US Army's 209 (Coast Artillery) Regiment which manned local gunsites for a time in 1942. The regiment had left New York on 11 May 1942, two days after his eighteenth birthday.

> I was a fraudulent enlistment as I lied about my age . . . We were part of the 1st

> Armored Div. As I recall the ship [the *Queen Mary*] was loaded to capacity with the division and attached troops. . . .
>
> We anchored off Gurroch and boarded a small ship to take us to Belfast. I remember marching to board buses and not too friendly people watching us. We were then taken to Palace Barracks, got settled in, and underwent a period of training by British soldiers in manning gunsites, aircraft recognition etc. it was very odd to us to have to put up blackout screens in order to get some sleep as the nights were very short.
>
> We then went to Magilligan Point . . . and did some gunnery [training]. Sometime during our stay . . . we did man a gunsite just outside of Londonderry at Sheriffs Mont, very close to the border. . . .
>
> As for personal feelings they were mixed. Being of Irish descent it was strange to us Irish as to what the big fuss was about the Protestants and Catholics. During Orange Day, we were at Londonderry then, we were restricted to the gunsite. However, we were never bothered by either side.

Ted Latta, a Technical Sergeant and a Crew Chief – head mechanic – on the P38s of 82nd Fighter Group, wrote a short account of his time at Eglinton with his impressions of the area and the food available when the group arrived there.

> ... our barracks were Quonset Huts down both sides of a company street. At the far end was the Airman's Ablutions (bathhouse) and the latrine.
>
> We settled into a semblance of camplife on a British air station to await the arrival of our P38s . . . 0ur first mess call on the RAF base happened to be Tea. We were served fresh bread, jam and margarine and tea laced with milk and sugar. Not bad for a bunch of hungry GIs, but it was all downhill from there.
>
> . . . In my own ramblings I came across the post gym with a sign over the door, 'You must be wearing Plimsoles to enter'. It took me a while to decipher that plimsoles were gym shoes. Ah – the colourful English language! A boot was the trunk of a car, a spanner was a Crescent Wrench and a Green Grocer sold only vegetables.
>
> Next door to the gym was the NAAFI, the English version of the USO. In the hut the local women sold tea and cakes. I . . . ordered a pot of tea and proceeded to load my plate with cookies and cakes. I settled down to enjoy myself only to find that they all had the flavour of GI laundry soap. I found out they had used sheep tallow for shortening. So much for the NAAFI.

To improve the food situation Ted Latta and his friends bought up the meagre stock of a local grocery shop and then raided a potato field by moonlight. The plants were dug up, 'depotatoed' and replanted.

They were allowed leave passes to 'Eglinton, Limavady, Ballymena, Portrush and Londonderry' and travelled by double-deck bus to towns where they were able to see how the civilian population was fighting the war.

> We located . . . the American Red Cross in downtown Londonderry on the second floor of a building on the main street. We were able to buy a cup of coffee and a doughnut there and to get directions to the various sights in the area.
>
> I remember some of us found an Irish Pub that served meals. The meal consisted of a bowl of potatoes about the size of golf balls. They were cooked in their skins and served with margarine. The spuds were peeled with your pocket knife and garnished with that mutton tallow margarine coloured to resemble butter. Another dish served was sausages made from sawdust and a plant called

> bloodroot. This was the first ersatz food we had. Our dreams at night were of ham and eggs, steak and real butter.

Even for Thanksgiving Day, when the Americans had hoped that a special meal might be provided, the treat consisted of 'a boiled kidney on a china plate surrounded by a yellow liquid'. Then, at last, an American Mess was set up and US rations became available as sufficient supplies were arriving in the UK. When the Mess opened and the group's men had their first American food in months 'C rations never tasted so good'. Any complainers were threatened with banishment to the British mess; 'no-one was so exiled'.

Sailing into Lough Foyle was always a pleasant experience. Many sailors remembered the green hillsides with cattle grazing and people waving as their ships steamed upriver. Robert L Hines was a Coast Guard sailor on board USS *Marchand* (DE-249), flagship of a six-strong Coast Guard-manned escort division.

> Londonderry was a very welcome 'Liberty' following 2 Murmansk, Russia runs. . . . I do recall visiting Northern Ireland as a happy and exciting experience.
>
> First, and most of all, I remember the children. Each Liberty several shipmates and myself would carry a large grocery bag of chocolate candy ashore and we felt like the Pied Piper as the children would follow us while we emptied the bags. . . .
>
> I also remember the churches . . . We attended worship services and we gave a pint of blood, so maybe a spot of my blood is still coursing through some Irishman's veins.
>
> I remember rain! Believe it or not it rained on every Liberty I made in Londonderry. One of the few places I had the opportunity to wear my Navy overcoat in lieu of the proverbial 'Pea Jacket'.

The rain was a surprise to many Americans, some of whom saw more rain in a day in Derry than in several years at home. Such was the impression made by the climate that an edition of Stars and Stripes, the US forces' newspaper included a cartoon with the caption: 'Patrick O'Shamrock of Ballybaloney distinctly remembers a day without rain, recorded in 1898". Charlie Gallagher recalled in his book *Acorns and Oak Leaves* that, after two days of continuous rain, one American serviceman devised a theory about the barrage balloons around the city: they were to 'keep this Goddam place from sinking'.

> 'Nine months winter and three months bad weather make up the year here', was the opinion of several others, but the piece de resistance came from a disgruntled, frustrated Chief Petty Officer. 'Lough Foyle' he said 'is the ass-hole of Northern Ireland and Derry is fourteen miles up it'.

Among the earliest US Navy ships to arrive at Lisahally was the destroyer tender USS *Melville*, which docked on 31 January 1942. One of its crew, John A Anders, later a lieutenant-commander, was transferred from the *Melville* to NOB, Londonderry on 1 April. Anders remained in the city until August 1943 'when I was transferred to Comdr, Naval Forces, Europe in London'.

> When I first arrived at NOB Londonderry I lived at the Springtown Camp and later at Aberfoyle House in Londonderry. I believe that the Royal Navy took it [Aberfoyle] over as quarters for US Naval Officers, and [it] was the home of the McFarlands.

> My stay in Derry was most pleasant and I have fond memories of many local families it was my good fortune to meet.

Anders is just one of many US servicemen with a similar happy recall of wartime service in the city. Many made close friends with local families; some, like John Tomassetti, met their future wives there.

> I arrived in Belfast on March 2, 1942 and arrived in Derry in the very early morning hours of March 3, 1942 with the US Navy Destroyer Repair Unit. (Advance Destroyer Base #1).
>
> I was quartered at Springtown until the latter part of August 1944, when we dismantled the repair base and came back to the States. . . .
>
> My wife is from Derry. Her name was Elizabeth McCallion and she lived at 16 Glenview Ave., Derry.

Relations with local people were generally good: the Americans' genial nature, and their kindness to children, made them very popular. In local dance halls they were received with mixed feelings: the womenfolk liked them but the men felt that the Americans were taking their women away; the friction could lead to fights which sometimes required intervention by the police, or naval shore patrols. But such friction was not restricted to the Americans: British servicemen also felt the hostility of local males who had lost girlfriends to men in uniform. Antipathy between Royal Navy personnel and US Marines based at Springtown led to a meeting between senior British and American officers on 12 September 1942 'to discuss measures to prevent further outbreaks of ill-feeling'.

The US authorities made special efforts to smooth relations between their personnel and local people. A handbook was published for servicemen being posted to Northern Ireland with sound advice on behaviour and local customs. This book, *A Pocket Guide to Northern Ireland*, included a warning about homemade alcohol which might be offered to servicemen in rural areas.

> . . . you may be offered an illicit concoction known as 'poteen'. This is a moonshine whiskey made out of potato wash. Watch it. It's dynamite.

The writer was obviously unaware that the 'concoction' might just as easily be offered in towns. Also included in the guide was advice on buying 'rounds' in pubs so that US servicemen would not give offence by 'a refusal to treat and be treated'. Not all the alcohol available in the pubs was to American taste, as C J Hickey discovered.

> In Londonderry there was a pub modelled after an American saloon. The owner had lived in Philadelphia for a number of years before returning to Ireland. The stock did not contain any whiskey or American beer, so most of us drank Stout with either port or sherry wine added to soften the flavour. I had my share of it and must confess that I felt as if I had a mouth full of cotton for days after. The good thing about this experience is that I did not over drink until after VJ day but that was a different ship, city and story.

Hickey also recounted an incident from his first trip to Derry in December 1943 that showed how relations with other Allied forces could be strained.

> We had been moored about three days when a large fist fight broke out between our crew and the Brits. I think that the Canadians had a fight with them the day before and our sympathies lay with the Canadians who seemed to be getting short shrift from the Brits. [What] ignited our fight was, . . . as I recall, several of the *Enright's* men were promised the rum ration [Royal Navy personnel were given a daily rum ration while US ships were 'dry'] in return for cigarettes. There was either real or imagined renegation plus the fact that several of the Brits were found in suspicious circumstances by several personal lockers, leaving the suspicion of theft.

Vance Crockett recalled a long running feud between American and British sailors arising from an incident during which a sailor was thrown over what appeared to be a low wall on Bonds Hill in the Waterside and fell more than twelve feet on the other side, sustaining severe injuries. For many weeks British and Canadian sailors fought American sailors in the streets with each successive escort group or division that arrived taking on the gauntlet from its predecessors. It required intervention from the most senior British and American officers in the city with threats of drastic disciplinary action to end the feud.

There was also friction between some local people and the Americans. Pig breeders in the area blamed the Americans for an outbreak of swine fever in the autumn of 1942. Discussions were held between local service representatives, both British and American, on 30 September about the disposal of 'messing by-products' in the area. The meeting was attended by the Inspector of Messing By Products of British Troops, Northern Ireland who agreed to approach the Ministry of Agriculture about proposals 'to safeguard pig breeders against further outbreaks of swine fever considered due to swill from US Service sources'.

Not all US servicemen had happy memories to take home. The story of the US Army's Sergeant Clipsham, who had the unenviable distinction of being the first US serviceman to be court-martialled in the United Kingdom, is told in Appendix 6. Another American, a sailor from an escort destroyer, found himself arraigned before a 'kangaroo' court in Derry, accused of attempting to rape a local girl. He was highly relieved by the intervention of members of the shore patrol who rescued him in the nick of time from an angry mob that intended to hang him from a lamp-post. Needless to say, that particular sailor was glad to say 'goodbye' to the city.

Many Royal Navy sailors had especially fond memories of the city and some of them found local wives, settling down to live in the city after the war. Most had seen Derry for the first time from an escort ship as it sailed up the Foyle towards the port. Donald Macintyre summed up their feelings when he wrote

> Londonderry was a land 'flowing with milk and honey' for us, where such unheard of luxuries as steaks could be had in the restaurants and butter in lumps instead of thin slivers. After the scene of smoking ruin at Liverpool, Londonderry's peaceful air, where people would probably show you the scene of the explosion of 'the bomb', was a benison. It sometimes made going to sea to face the winter gales all the harder. As one slipped down the narrow river, peaceful little sheltered cottages passed within biscuit toss. The blue peat smoke rose lazily into the air and one envied the owners their warm fireside and quiet night ahead of them. A corner of the river would be rounded, the wind would start keening

Commander E H Chavasse, a native of west Cork, who has commanded 2nd (Canadian) Escort Group from HMS *Broadway*. In May 1943 his Group escorted convoy HX 237 across the Atlantic, sinking U89 and U456 en route (Chapter 5). (IWM: A23399)

Commanding officers of three ships of 7th Escort Group which sank two U-boats in November 1943. L to R: Lieutenant Commander C R Hart, DSC and Bar, of HMS *Vidette*; Commander P W Gretton, OBE, DSC, of HMS *Duncan*; and Lieutenant Commander J Plomer, DSC, of HMS *Sunflower*. Hart later commanded 21st Escort Group which escorted the first group of surrendered U-boats into Lisahally on 14 May 1945. Grettons son is currently an Admiral while Plomer was a Royal Canadian Navy Volunteer Reserve officer. (IWM: A20147)

Congratulations! February 1945 and Commodore Simpson reads a signal from Admiral Sir Ma Horton, Commander-in-Chief, Western Approaches to members of 10th Escort Group which had just accounted for two 'probable' and one 'possible' U-boat sinkings in the North Atlantic. (IWM: A 274080

Admiral Sir max K Horton, KCB, DSO, CinC, Western Approaches on the bridge of HMS *Philante* during escort group anti-submarine exercises. In the centre of the photograph is *Philante's* commanding officer, Captain A J Baker Cresswell, DSO. (IWM: A17821)

Surrendered U-boats tied up at the Royal Navy jetty at Lisahally on 24 May 1945. The photograph was taken from t he observer's position in a Swordfish on the Mac Wing from Maydown. The US Navy jetty can be seen behind the RN jetty in this picture. (IW: A28892)

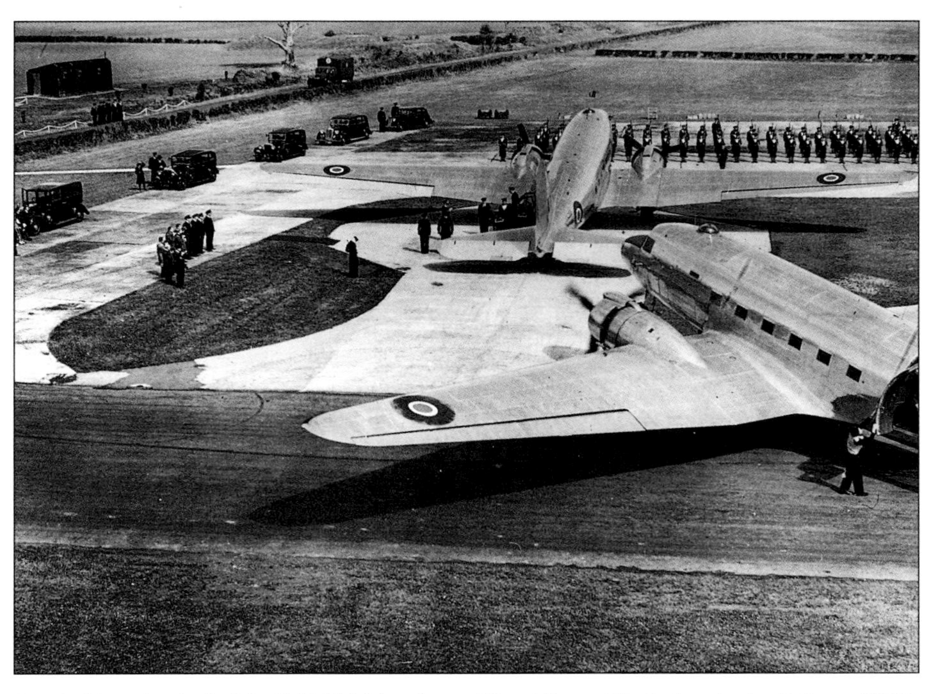

Royal visit to the city in July 1945. TM King George VI and Queen Elizabeth arrived at Eglinton (HMS *Gannet*) in a RAF Dakota. A reception party and guard of honour await while the cavalcade of official cars is drawn up to the left of the photograph. A strip of red carpet can be seen across the grass to the left of the first Dakota. (IWM: A29827)

Windy corner. Three US sailors on the corner of Waterloo Place and William Street. The railings in the foreground, in front of Littlewoods, were there until 1967. (Robert L Hines)

Great to see ya! Happy children from the Rosemount area pose for the camera and candies from crewmen of the USS Marchand. In the right background can be seen an air raid shelter while the large building to the left is the Rosemount Factory. The house in the centre background was the author's maternal grandparents' home. (Robert L Hines)

Termon Street in the Waterside looking across the river. The white paint on the Morrison air raid shelter can be clearly seen in this picture. (Robert L Hines)

A happy sailor takes the reins of a very sedate means of transport while on liberty in the city. (Robert L Hines)

RAF Maydown in August 1942 before the airfield was handed over to the Admiralty to become HMS *Shrike*. Both the Royal Navy and US Navy jetties at Lisahally can be clearly seen while a number of barrage balloon sites are also identifiable. (RAF Museum)

Spitfires. By the end of March, 134 had left but 152 stayed until mid-August, their replacements being the US Army Air Corps' 52nd Fighter Group, which also operated Spitfires.

The Americans disposed two squadrons, one at Eglinton and the other at Maydown. They had arrived because of General Eisenhower's wish to have US troops relieved of ground defence commitments in Northern Ireland with US units taking over air defence. The Group's Spitfires were supplied by Britain, on Reverse Lend-Lease, until such time as their own American-built machines arrived by sea in the UK.

On 7 August the Group's 2nd Fighter Squadron deployed to Maydown from where, next day, the squadron, with part of No.152 Squadron, which was still in residence at Eglinton, put up a 16-Spitfire escort for a convoy: this was 52nd Fighter Group's first operational mission.

On 11 August 5th Fighter Squadron was declared operational at sunrise, allowing 152 Squadron to stand down from active operations, although it remained available to assist the Americans until its departure on 16 August.

A week later two sections of 5th Fighter Squadron were ordered into the air to intercept a hostile over Donegal but, by the time they arrived, 504 Squadron Hurricanes had shot down the intruder. Over the next few weeks the 52nd carried out convoy escort patrols with no incidents, proving the old dictum that war is long periods of boredom interspersed with short spells of frenetic activity. The group was still flying its British Spitfires, painted with American stars, when it left Eglinton for a base in England. For a short spell there were no American flyers at Eglinton but, on 4 October, the advance party of 82nd Fighter Group arrived; once again a squadron, 97th Fighter, was deployed to Maydown. The group had some Spitfires until it received its complement of Lockheed P38 Lightnings, the first of which began to arrive from assembly units at Speke, Abbotsinch and Burtonwood in November. Tragically, one was lost together with its pilot when the plane developed problems on approach to Eglinton and crashed into a nearby hillside.

The group flew practice long-range bomber escort missions with its P38s in company with B17 Flying Fortresses, as well as routine patrols off the north coast. Finally, at the end of December, 82nd Fighter Group left Eglinton to join 12th Air Force in North Africa.

The departure of the Americans virtually marked the end of Eglinton and Maydown as fighter stations. On 4 January 1943 Maydown closed to allow improvement work to be carried out and Eglinton played host to some aircraft detached from No.501 Squadron at Ballyhalbert for air defence. These were the last operational RAF fighters to fly from Eglinton: the threat to the northwest had diminished considerably, allowing No.920 Balloon Squadron to be disbanded in February 1943, and there was no further need for a large number of fighters to be based in the area. And so Eglinton and Maydown entered on a new phase of their lives, being handed over to the Admiralty as Fleet Air Arm stations from 1 May 1943.

The sight of Spitfires in the skies around the city undoubtedly invoked thoughts of RAF Fighter Command's struggle against the Luftwaffe over southern Britain in the summer of 1940, the Battle of Britain, when Churchill's immortal 'Few' had forced the Germans to end their daylight offensive.

One side effect of the Battle of Britain was an unexpected surge in the number of individuals wishing to contribute to the purchase of Spitfires. This led to some 1,300 'presentation' Spitfires joining the RAF, all paid for by voluntary contributions from individuals or companies throughout the United Kingdom and beyond. The slogan 'Buy a Spitfire' became a catchphrase and money poured in from India, Canada, Australia, South Africa, Mexico, Peru, Argentina and Columbia, among others. Presentation aircraft had been known in the Great War but the extent of the phenomenon after August 1940 took the government by surprise; in fact, the Air Ministry would have preferred it not to have happened.

Many companies and wealthy individuals paid for aircraft but for the less well-off there were a number of schemes: redheads were invited to contribute towards a Spitfire called *Gingerbread* flown by the flame-haired Australian 'Ginger' Lacey while girls called Dorothy could contribute to a machine of the same name.

But by the far the most common type of presentation was by towns and communities, often led by a local or regional newspaper. In this fashion Northern Ireland, led by the Belfast Telegraph Fund, provided no less than seventeen Spitfires for Fighter Command. The first Telegraph Spitfire to be delivered to the RAF bore the name *Londonderry*, although it was paid for by the county rather than the city. To distinguish between the origins of Spitfires from Londonderry and County Londonderry the city's presentation machine bore the name *City of Derry*; this was P7839, the 58th presentation Spitfire which was delivered to the RAF on 1 January 1941.

Built at Castle Bromwich, *City of Derry*, a Spitfire Mark II, was allocated to No.74 (Tiger) Squadron, one of the RAF's most famous units, on 5 March 1941. It was engaged on a number of patrols, sustaining battle damage on 21 March from which it returned to service six days later. On 7 April P/O Howard in *City of Derry* damaged a Messerschmitt Bf109 while his wingman, Sergeant Rogowski, destroyed another Bf109. Three days later, Howard was with another wingman, P/O Chester, who also shot down a Bf109 but was killed when he crashed on landing.

At the end of April, *City of Derry* received serious damage in combat and was removed to a Civilian Repair Unit (CRU) for repair. On 2 June it was accepted by 8th Maintenance Unit who issued the machine to No.308 (Krakowski) Squadron, a Polish unit, on 9 July.

The Krakowski squadron was based at Speke, now Liverpool Airport, but on 22 July it transferred its aircraft to another Polish unit, 315 (Deblinski) Squadron which then moved to Northolt near London. F/Lt Mickiewicz flew *City of Derry* on a patrol south of Dover on 31 July while P/O Nowak took her a week later over Nieuport, St Omer and Gravelines. The squadron's first major aerial combat occurred over Fruges on 14 August. In an intensive action with Bf109s 'Deblinski' destroyed eight enemy aircraft, claimed another 'possible' and one damaged. *City of Derry* was flown on this occasion by Sergeant Gruszynski. The action earned the squadron commendations from the Air Officer Commanding 11 Group and Fighter Command's chief.

The next day, 15 August, the Poles celebrated their success: the squadron's record book notes: 'it being the Feast of the Polish Forces, Holy Mass was celebrated in the hangar. There was no flying'.

P/O Nowak flew *City of Derry* again on 19 August when RAF machines came under heavy enemy air attack over France. 315 Squadron formed a defensive circle and Nowak shot down and destroyed one of the attacking Bf109s. *City of Derry* saw one final sweep with 'Deblinski' before 315 began to re-equip with the newer Spitfire V which was superseding the II. On 11 September 1941 *City of Derry* was transferred to 610 Squadron and, less than a month later, on 4 October, was totally destroyed in a flying accident.

The north-west's other presentation Spitfire, P7683, *Londonderry*, had a longer life. Also a Castle Bromwich Mark II, it was only the eleventh presentation Spitfire to be delivered. It was issued to No.603 Squadron, which had the distinction of having shot down the first German aircraft over Britain in the Second World War, at Drem in Scotland on 22 December 1940.

Six months later *Londonderry* was transferred to the famous 111 Squadron at Hornchurch in Essex. Moving to Driffield, Yorkshire, the squadron then transferred to North Weald, Essex, from where it flew on convoy patrols, Army co-operation exercises and offensive sweeps over France. Various pilots flew *Londonderry* in fifteen sweeps and six convoy patrols between 24 July and 28 August. Over Lille in northern France, on 19 August, Sergeant Smyth, piloting *Londonderry*, was credited with the 'probable' destruction of an enemy fighter.

Londonderry was damaged in late August and, after repair, was issued to 123 Squadron on 25 November with which it served until transfer to 58 Operational Training Unit on 12 March 1942. By then the Spitfire II was obsolescent and *Londonderry* spent the rest of its days in a training role until being destroyed in a flying accident on 19 August 1943.

The Spitfires had been paid for by small contributions building up through the co-ordinated efforts of the Belfast Telegraph: *City of Derry*, for example, was paid for by £3,000 raised in the city itself with the balance of the £5,000 needed to purchase a Spitfire coming from the Telegraph Fund.

Londonderry purchased another aircraft for the RAF in 1943 as a result of the Wings for Victory Campaign, a government-backed scheme, co-ordinated throughout the UK, in which participating communities were set a target on reaching which they were allowed to choose a representative aircraft. Having reached its target (details of which have not been discovered), Londonderry was allotted an Avro Lancaster Mark III, DV180, which was given the city's name. This was one of a batch of 200 Lancasters built and delivered by Metropolitan-Vickers between May and November 1943.

DV180, *Londonderry*, was assigned to No.103 Squadron of Bomber Command and took part in operations against Germany before being transferred to No.166 Squadron. While taking part in a 769-bomber raid on Berlin on the night of 20/21 January 1944, Londonderry went missing. It had undoubtedly fallen to German defences, either Flak (AA guns), or night-fighters; DV180 was one of 35 aircraft lost. It is likely that *Londonderry* fell to night-fighters as the German controllers had guided their fighters into the bomber stream early that night as it approached Berlin in a wide sweep from the north. The fighters stayed with the attacking bombers, scoring heavily until the force was well on its way home. At some stage in this aerial battle it seems that *Londonderry* fell to cannon-fire from a Luftwaffe night-fighter.

The life of a wartime aircraft is invariably quite short. So it was with the north-west's presentation machines but although the two Spitfires and the Lancaster had but brief service careers they all acquitted themselves well. No more could have been asked of them.

10

EVERYWHERE

THE city's strategic location was not its only contribution to the War. Local men, and women, volunteered to join the services; almost 3,000 Derrymen wore Royal Navy, Army or Royal Air Force uniform, with the largest single grouping in 9th (Londonderry) Heavy Anti-Aircraft Regiment, Royal Artillery (Supplementary Reserve).

The creation of a Northern Irish anti-aircraft brigade was first announced in July 1938. On 7 December 3rd AA Brigade officially came into being; it included two AA regiments, a searchlight regiment and supporting units. One AA regiment was to be raised in Belfast, the other in Londonderry, as 8th AA Regiment and 9th AA Regiment respectively.

Recruiting for 9th Regiment began in April 1939. Officers had already been commissioned and regular Royal Artillery personnel had arrived to fill key posts and conduct training. The regiment comprised a headquarters, based in huts in Ebrington Barracks, and four AA batteries: three were to be equipped with heavy guns and the fourth, based at Coleraine, with light guns; one heavy battery, 26 Battery, was to be raised in the Ballymena area. Battery designations were 24, 25 and 26 AA Batteries and 6 LAA Battery.

Recruiting was brisk with a flood of applicants to the recruiting office in the Northern Counties Hotel. Manpower came much faster than equipment and clothing: the first weapons to arrive were two Great War vintage 3-inch guns delivered on 29 April along with fire-control equipment. No live rounds were supplied; training was carried out with wooden rounds.

On 8 May 1939 the regiment moved to the newly built Caw Camp and training continued throughout the summer. A common, but inaccurate, perception in the regiment's home city is that they were Territorial Army soldiers: the brigade was part of the Supplementary Reserve, part of the Army's First Class Reserve. Soldiers of 9th Regiment were almost part of the Regular Army. This is further shown by the regiment's designation: there were only seven regular heavy anti-aircraft regiments and the two Northern Ireland-raised regiments became 8th and 9th Regiments; TA HAA regiments were numbered from 51st onwards. As a Supplementary Reserve formation 3rd AA Brigade was to join the British Expeditionary Force in France in late-1939.

However, the Derrymen of 9th Regiment moved overseas in November 1939, dispatched by the War Office, which retained responsibility for AA defences throughout the Empire, to Alexandria in Egypt, a principal anchorage of the Royal Navy's Mediterranean Fleet. They thus became the first reserve forces to deploy overseas in the Second World War.

At Alexandria, 9th Regiment was operational by the new year of 1940 and had been joined by 20 AA Battery, with twelve rather then eight guns; later, 5 HAA Battery of the Royal Malta Artillery increased regimental strength to five heavy batteries and a light battery: the latter was 5 LAA Battery from north Down, originally part of 8th AA Regiment, rather than 6 LAA Battery from Coleraine.

When Italy declared war, in June 1940, 9th (Londonderry) HAA Regiment, as it had officially become, controlled 44 HAA guns and twelve LAA guns, virtually all British AA artillery resources in the Middle East. Not only was it the largest AA regiment in the Army, it was soon to become the most widely dispersed gunner regiment. In the summer of 1940, 25 Battery went to The Sudan from where it detached sections to Aden and later to support General Cunningham's forces liberating Eritrea.

The peregrinations of 25 Battery had begun in early May when half the battery had moved to El Daba in the Western Desert under command of 7th Armoured Division, whose desert rat symbol was soon to achieve considerable fame. The same sections moved to Sudan in late-June, followed by the remainder of the battery some weeks later.

The Londonderry Regiment provided the backbone of Alexandria defences until March 1942 but 25 Battery spent very little time there. They remained in Sudan until 1941 but their return to Alexandria, on Easter Sunday morning, coincided with Rommel's breakthrough into Egypt at the Halfaya Pass and so they were immediately ordered up the desert to Mersa Matruh, at that time Egypt's last line of defence. Thus began a spell of almost six months in the desert with duties varying from defending Matruh to protecting forward landing airstrips of the RAF and the South African Air Force, from whom they received special thanks.

Defending airstrips meant receiving direct attention from German and Italian aircraft in the form of strafing attacks. Towards the end of their days in the desert they came close to being captured in a two-pronged German attack near Halfaya, but fortunately the German supply column with its fuel lorries was destroyed by RAF aircraft.

On 10 March 1942 9th Regiment finally left Alexandria where they had engaged over a hundred air raids and had destroyed at least five enemy aircraft. More importantly, however, not one ship in Alexandria harbour had been damaged by bombing – a distinction which 25 Battery also achieved at Port Sudan. The Royal Navy was especially appreciative and there were many tributes to the regiment's prowess as it moved out to the Canal Zone.

From the Canal Zone, 9th Regiment moved to Palestine in the summer of 1942 to join Ninth Army to defend against a possible German invasion through the Caucasus. The batteries deployed to cover long-range bomber airfields and carried out defence exercises; soldiers also had the opportunity to see some of the Holy Land's historic sights.

By early-November the threat from the north had receded and the regiment was ordered to join Eighth Army, leaving Palestine for Egypt on a long trek after Montgomery's westward advancing army which had defeated PanzerArmee Afrika at El Alamein. The main task facing the Derry Boys was a special request from the Royal Navy who had asked that 9th (Londonderry)

11

VICTORY

FROM May 1943 the tide of war had swung against the U-boats. Although they had been extracting a heavy toll from Allied merchant shipping as late as March 1943, when it appeared that the struggle could go either way, the much improved Allied anti-submarine effort ensured that in the last two years of war in Europe the U-boats were more often the hunted rather than the hunter. That is not to say that they were no longer a menace: U-boat activities threatened the Normandy operations in June 1944 when groups from the Londonderry Escort Force deployed to the English Channel to protect the invasion armada. In the closing months of war U-boats audaciously operated in British and Irish waters and menaced shipping in the Irish Sea; passenger ships sailing between Northern Ireland and Scotland did so with a naval escort. But the U-boats operated at great risk to themselves and the price paid in boats sunk and crews killed was high.

That the German submarines were still a menace can be demonstrated by a walk through Londonderry city cemetery where a war graves' plot holds the remains of two sailors from HMS *Redmill*, torpedoed in Donegal Bay on 27 April 1945 with the loss of twenty-seven lives. *Redmill*, a Captain-class frigate (the RN designation for lend-lease destroyer escorts supplied by the US), was towed into the Foyle. The U-boat which torpedoed her was subsequently sunk by *Redmill's* escort group, the Belfast-based 21st, which earlier in the war had operated out of Londonderry.

When Dönitz, who succeeded Hitler as Führer, unconditionally surrendered all German forces to the Allies on 4 May 1945, the submarines of the U-boat fleet were ordered to surrender to the nearest Allied ships. Some captains chose to scuttle their boats – over 200 were destroyed in this fashion – but others complied with Dönitz's order, surfacing to signal their surrenders to nearby ships and be escorted to British ports.

Although Germany had surrendered and the war in Europe was over, the Allies were still engaged against the Japanese in the Pacific and in Burma. That war ended with the atomic bombing of Hiroshima and Nagasaki in August 1945 and the last Derrymen on active service began to be shipped home. Many had died in the war in the east, of whom some perished between VE day in May and VJ in August 1945. For their families the cheerfulness of the celebrations of VE Day was tinged with regret.

To mark the end of the U-boat war and the part played by Londonderry in that final victory, Admiral Sir Max Horton decided to travel to Lisahally where surrendered U-boats were to be tied up before disposal. On 14 May 1945 Horton stood on the jetty at Lisahally, where so many sailors had landed after gruelling trips across the Atlantic facing the menace of the U-boats, and watched as eight boats, with Royal Navy guards on their skeleton German crews, were escorted in by 21st Escort Group ships. The first to dock was U-802. As the German officers stepped ashore formal naval salutes were exchanged but there was no handshaking. Although as professional naval officers, and submariners, Horton and the Germans would have respected each other, a press image of friendly informality would have been offensive to those thousands who had lost loved ones to the U-boats in the long days of the Battle of the Atlantic. Among the group with Horton at Lisahally were several Wrens who had been stationed in Derry; their presence marked their contribution to the battle. Wearing plain clothes and adopting a low profile was the head of Irish intelligence, Colonel Dan Bryan; the Irish role in the defeat of the U-boats had been important but was obscured by the arguments over Irish neutrality. Bryan's presence indicated Britain's appreciation of Ireland's support.

How important was Derry? In the early days of the battle it had been a vital base for the Allied navies, providing an extra degree of cover that had ensured the survival of many merchant ships. It continued to play that strategic role throughout the Atlantic campaign with the air bases along the Foyle added to the port itself and the Lisahally anchorage. And the training carried out at the naval base was invaluable in producing the standard of operating professionalism and co-operation between surface and air escorts that led to defeat for the U-boats. Horton's presence at Lisahally on 14 May is the surest indicator of the city's importance but there were subsequent further indicators.

In March 1941, as the Londonderry naval base was growing in size, an Admiralty officer wrote that Londonderry and Scotland would be the 'naval bases of the future (i.e. after the war)'. And so it transpired: after the war anti-submarine training was virtually concentrated on the Foyle with the establishment of the Joint Anti-Submarine School (JASS) at Ebrington Barracks which was retained by the Royal Navy and commissioned as HMS *Sea Eagle*. The RAF established a JASS Flight at Ballykelly and the Fleet Air Arm trained its carrier-borne anti-submarine crews at Eglinton until 1958 while an anti-submarine group of ships was based in the city as the Derry Squadron. NATO escort groups visited regularly to take part in exercises while anti-submarine aircraft of various NATO nations could often be seen in the skies above the city.

Perhaps the most regular visitors were Royal Canadian and US Navy ships while Dutch, Norwegian and French ships often brought memories of wartime days. US, Canadian, and Dutch aircraft were to be seen overhead while, under the sea off the mouth of Lough Foyle, the Soviet Navy kept a submarine permanently on station to observe and report on the activities of NATO nations. Had there been a Third World War, the Greenland-Iceland-UK Gap would have played a major role in any new battle of the Atlantic and, once again, the city on the Foyle would have been thrust into prominence.

In 1970 HMS *Sea Eagle* was decommissioned and, the following year, RAF Ballykelly closed as an air base, bringing to an end the role that the city and the river had played in grand strategy since the summer of 1940.

In the aftermath of war there were many tangible reminders of those years in and around the city. AA gunsites could be seen for many years along with balloon sites, some air-raid shelters and the yellow signs pointing the way to First Aid Posts and Gas Cleansing Stations. Now only two of the gunsites survive, at Sherrif's Mountain and Mabuoy, while a single faded yellow sign on Foyle Road under Craigavon Bridge is the sole remaining marking of a First Aid Post. There is another reminder that is not recognised as such: at Cloughglass estate, off Northland Road, stand a number of aluminium Hawksley bungalows, erected in the late 1940s. The Hawksleys were among several patterns of factory-built houses produced by aircraft manufacturing companies to meet the post-war demand for housing. Londonderry Corporation chose the Hawksley, a product of the Hawker Siddeley Company which owned the Armstrong-Whitworth, Avro, Gloster and Hawker aircraft companies, for Cloughglass and a number of streets in the new Creggan estate. The bungalows were recycled from aircraft scrapped by the Royal Air Force after the war. Their aluminium structures are, therefore, well into their second, but much more peaceful, lives. If walls could speak those bungalows might have some very interesting stories to tell of their first lives.

The importance of the city to the war effort is not generally recognised locally. Perhaps the city's peripheral location in Europe has something to do with that; perhaps there was a desire to put the unpleasantness of war behind. It could also be argued that a city with a nationalist majority population had no wish to remember being such a vital part in Britain's war effort and in Britain's survival, although it must be remembered that the contribution of Derry's Catholics was as important as that of the city's Protestants and death was no respecter of religious affiliations. Perhaps also it could be a collective application of what psychologists refer to as the forty-year block, a closing out of awful experiences from the memory for a period of roughly four decades. Whatever the reason for earlier lack of interest in the war years, there has more recently been a growing interest in that aspect of the city's history. Hopefully, this book will help to satisfy part of that interest.

Appendix 1

TAKE THESE MEN

IN all three fighting services Derrymen gained distinction and a book could be devoted to their achievements. However, since space precludes that, a selection of three distinguished Derrymen has been made to exemplify the part the city's sons played in the war.

Among the first local men to achieve distinction was a naval officer, Sub-Lieutenant John Tillie, who was awarded the Distinguished Service Cross (DSC) after the Battle of Narvik in 1940. On 10 April 2nd Destroyer Flotilla sailed up the Vest Fiord in a blinding snowstorm forcing its way into the inner harbour of Narvik to wreak considerable damage on enemy shipping. As the flotilla steamed back down the fiord, HMS *Hotspur*, badly damaged, stopped. It was then that Tillie showed his courage:

> Though himself wounded, he rallied the survivors from his two guns' crews and opened a rapid and accurate fire on the enemy, causing them to keep their distance until the *Hostile* and *Havock* could return to cover the *Hotspur's* withdrawal.

Three days later a further raid put all German ships in Narvik out of action. Allied troops landed and Narvik was recaptured from the Germans on 28 May; sadly, the operation was a diversion to distract the Germans from the Allied intention to evacuate Norway.

John Tillie went on to earn a Bar to his DSC in the Mediterranean with Force H where 'his skill and coolness during the tracking down of an Italian submarine largely contributed to its ultimate destruction'.

Following that operation, Tillie saw considerable arduous service in the eastern Mediterranean, including the evacuation of Crete in May 1941. Later that year he was involved in the relief of the besieged port of Tobruk and escorted convoys in the Mediterranean, during which he assisted in the destruction of another enemy submarine. He died at sea as a result of enemy action.

The first local airman to gain distinction also did so early in the war. Andrew Woodrow Dunn, from Springtown, a Pilot-Officer in Bomber Command's No.77 Squadron, flew a Whitley Mk V, an aircraft with which his squadron was first to be equipped, in several early operations over Germany. On these missions Bomber Command, forbidden to drop bombs, was restricted to dropping leaflets aimed at convincing German civilians that the war was a pointless exercise. The leaflet dropping was certainly pointless, leading one wag to observe that its only result was to provide the Reich with generous supplies of toilet paper.

Pilot Officer Dunn also took part in a number of reconnaissance missions until, in the spring of 1940, Whitleys began to be used in their intended role. Dunn's squadron was involved in a number of 'firsts': the first attack on an enemy land target, the first major attack on mainland Germany and, on the night after Italy declared war on Britain, the first bombing raid on Italy.

During a raid against Germany's industrial heartland, the Ruhr, in June 1940, Andrew Dunn demonstrated the gallantry that won him the Distinguished Flying Cross (DFC). On the run in to the target his Whitley was subjected to heavy anti-aircraft gunfire over a period of fifteen minutes. The aircraft was hit several times and was then attacked by a Messerschmitt Bf109 fighter. The 109's first attack destroyed the Whitley's inter-communication equipment as well as wounding both the observer/navigator and the wireless operator.

Lack of an intercom meant that the tail gunner could not tell Dunn that the Messerschmitt was coming in for a second attack. Fortunately, the gunner was able to shoot the fighter down, but not before it had opened fire on the Whitley and damaged an engine.

In spite of all this trauma, Andrew Dunn pressed home his attack to drop his bombs in the target area before turning for home. With two injured crewmen and only one engine it was to be a hazardous journey. After three and a half hours they crossed the North Sea at only 400 feet. In spite of their injuries the navigator and the wireless operator continued to perform their duties and were thus able to ensure that the pilot could get as near home as possible.

But it proved an impossible task for the crippled Whitley to make England. Dunn was forced to crash-land the bomber in the sea close to the English coast and the crew were rescued speedily. For showing 'the greatest determination, courage and gallantry throughout this operation' Dunn was awarded the DFC.

But, like John Tillie, Andrew Dunn was not to survive the war. On the night of 23 September 1940 he took off from Driffield, Yorkshire, at the controls of Whitley P5046, (O-Orange) on an operation against Berlin. Bomber Command had assembled a force of almost 130 Whitleys, Wellingtons and Hampdens to bomb military installations, railway yards, power stations and factories in and around Berlin. Nothing was heard from Dunn's aircraft after take-off and, next morning, when the bombers returned to their bases P5046 was not among them.

No trace was ever found of Andrew Dunn's plane; the Royal Air Force presumed it 'to have crashed into the sea' with the loss of all five crew members.

In the jungles of Burma, as British troops retreated before the Japanese onslaught, the first DSO of the campaign was awarded to a Derryman, Lieutenant-Colonel Keegan whose battalion, 2nd King's Own Yorkshire Light Infantry (KOYLI), had been the first British battalion to engage the Japanese in Burma. Keegan earned the DSO after his battalion's performance in crossing the Sittang river.

The Sittang was a major obstacle to the withdrawal of 17th Division which had to cross a single bridge on 22 February 1942. This was a single-track railway bridge which had been planked to carry motor transport. There was confusion at the crossing point and the bridge was blocked for two hours when a driver panicked and slid off the track. The situation was one of near chaos and when Japanese troops burst out of the jungle during the morning there was a feeling of panic. Fighting raged throughout that night. The divisional commander, believing that most of his division had crossed the Sittang, ordered the bridge to be blown up; this was done at 5.30am on 23 February. But most of 17th Division was still on the far bank and an improvised ferry had been knocked out the day before.

As the Japanese closed in, small groups of British, Indian, Gurkha and Burmese soldiers tried to cross the river. Among these were the remnants of 2nd KOYLI. Their regimental history recounts what happened:

> . . . as dawn broke on 23 February 1942 morale in the battalion was not high. Panic was very near. . . . The river presented an extraordinary spectacle. An air of subdued urgency bordering on panic hung over everything. Hundreds of British, Indian and Gurkha troops were constructing rafts from anything which might conceivably float . . . low-flying Jap aircraft cruised up and down the river machine-gunning swimmers.

Colonel Keegan was, by contrast, a picture of calmness: encouraging survivors to swim or raft across the river, he held on with two companies of KOYLIs and some Burma Rifles soldiers until nightfall, fighting off the attackers. After dark he had the wounded rafted over in a three-hour operation. Keegan, who had been wounded during the course of the day, was among the last to cross, together with the commanding officer of a Gurkha battalion. His courage and cool nerve had done much to save the situation and to allow the safe withdrawal of much of 17th Division. Few DSOs have been better deserved.

Appendix 2

SHIPS based in city (with acknowledgements to Jim Colledge on whose original research the Royal and Royal Canadian Naval element of this Appendix is based):

On 9 December 1940 the Londonderry naval base was commissioned as HMS *Ferret*. Three former yachts, *Firefly*, *Aloha Moana* and *Onora*, successively acted as the nominal base ship under the title *Ferret* until the base decommissioned on 21 June 1947.

In August 1940 the depot ship *Titania* arrived in the city but left the following month. The depot ship *Sandhurst* then arrived but left in August 1941. Also in the summer of 1940 3rd Motor Launch (ML) Flotilla with MLs 121 to 128 arrived; MLs 124, 125 and 127 left in October but were replaced by MLs 129, 130 and 135. In November 1940 the strength of the base included 3rd ML Flotilla, five corvettes (*Anemone*, *Arabis*, *Clarkia*, *Gentian* and *Mallow*) and the examination services yacht *Clarinda*. When the base officially commissioned as HMS *Ferret* it was also playing host to its first Escort Groups, 1st and 2nd Escort Groups. The following table shows the Escort Groups operating from the port from December 1940 until the end of the war as they were constituted in January of each year.

January 1941:

1st EG: HM Ships Malcolm; Sabre; Skate (destroyers); Clarkia; Gladiolus; and Mallow (corvettes)

2nd EG: HM Ships Broke; Saladin; Sardonyx; Scimitar and Shikari (destroyers); Arabis; Anemone; Heliotrope and La Malouine (corvettes)

6th ML Flotilla: ML 152 (MLs 145 to 151 were awaited to join the flotilla)

Examination Service: Clarinda (yacht); Night Hawk; and Scarron (trawlers)

Anti-submarine trawlers: HM Ships Ayrshire; Man o'War; Northern Dawn; Northern Gem; Northern Pride; Northern Spray; Northern Wave; St Elstan; St Kenan; St Zeno; Vizalma and Vellard

January 1942:

1st EG: HM Ships Keppel; Lincoln; Venomous; Alisma; Bellwort; Dianella; Kingcup; Loosestrife and Sunflower

2nd EG: HM Ships Douglas; Leamington; Veteran; Abelia; Anemone; Asphodel; Thyme and Veronica

8th EG: HM Ships Malcolm; Newmarket; Watchman; Arabis; Dahlia; Monkswood; Petunia and Snowflake

20th EG: HM Ships Badsworth; Lamerton and Lauderdale

21st EG: HM Ships Sabre; Scimitar; Shikari; Skate; Saladin and Sardonyx

22nd EG: HM Ships Beverley; Ripley; Rockingham and Sherwood

40th EG: HM Ships Landguard; Culver; Lulworth; Bideford and Londonderry

41st EG: HM Ships Ibis; Enchantress; Aberdeen; Clare; Hartland and Walney

42nd EG: HM Ships Weston; Folkestone; Wellington; Gorleston; Sennen and Totland

43rd EG: HM Ships Rochester; Leith; Sandwich; Scarborough and Bradford

44th EG: HM Ships Egret; Fleetwood; Hastings; Banff; Fishguard and Philante (yacht)

Corvettes unallocated: Anchusa and Oxlip

Trawlers attached to Escort Groups: Lady Elsa; Man o'War; Northern Dawn and Wellard (all 1st EG); St Elstan; St Kenan; St Zeno and Vizalma (all 2nd EG); Northern Gem; Northern Pride; Northern Spray and Northern Wave (all 8th EG)

(Late in January 1942 the anti-submarine trawlers attached to 1st, 2nd and 8th Escort Groups were detached from those groups to form 45th, 46th and 47th Escort Groups)

109 Minesweeping Flotilla: 2 motor minesweepers

Miscellaneous vessels: 2 Examination Service vessels; 8 minesweeper drifters; 2 boom-defence trawlers; 3 tenders; 1 balloon vessel; and 1 air-sea rescue (ASR) trawler which was actually stationed in Killybegs, Co Donegal with the tacit agreement of the Irish government.

January 1943:

1st EG: HM Ships Hurricane; Watchman; Rockingham; Anchusa; Borage; Dahlia; Meadowsweet; Monkshood and Wallflower

4th EG: HM Ships Highlander; Winchelsea; Beverley; Abelia; Anemone; Asphodel; Clover; Pennywort and Snowflake

7th EG: HM Ships Chesterfield; Ripley; Alisma; Coreoposis; Jonquil; Loosestrife; and Sunflower

21st EG: HM Ships Sabre; Saladin; Sardonyx; Scimitar; Shikari; and Skate

24th EG: HM Ships Dianella; Lotus; Poppy and Starwort

25th (Canadian) EG: HM Ships Louisburg; Prestcott and Woodstock

27th (Canadian) EG: HM Ships Algoma; Calgary; Camrose; Kitchener; Moosejaw and Regina

28th EG: HM Ships Azalea; Coltsfoot; Geranium and Spiraea

40th EG: HM Ships Bideford; Hastings; Londonderry; Landguard; Lulworth; Kale; Moyola and Ness

42nd EG: HM Ships Folkestone; Wellington; Weston; Gorleston; Totland; Jed; Teviot; and Waveney

44th EG: HM Ships Clare; Egret; Exe; Test; Banff; Fishguard and Philante (yacht)

45th EG: HM Ships Pelican; Aberdeen; Lowestoft; Sennen; Rother; Spey; Tay; Wear and Bradford

Special EG: HM Ships Douglas; Keppel; Badsworth and Lauderdale

Unallocated: HM Ships Cygnet; Whimbrel; Woodpecker and Lagan

139 Minesweeper Group with 3 trawlers; 1 yacht and 2 trawlers with the Examination Service; 7 minesweeping drifters; 2 tugs; the ASR trawler at Killbegs; HMS Foxglove, an anti-aircraft guardship (arrived May 1943 as 'Advanced Base & AA Guardship') moored downstream as part of the base's anti-aircraft defences, and 7 miscellaneous vessels

January 1944:

1st EG: HM Ships Wanderer; Watchman; Glenarm; Borage; Dahlia; Wallflower; and Portchester Castle

1st (Canadian) EG: HM Ships Assiniboine; St Laurent; Forester; Ettrick; Celandine; Agnassiz; Fredericton; Galt; Giffard and Halifax

2nd (Canadian) Escort Group: HM Ships Gatineau; Icarus; St Catherine; Chilliwack; Drumheller; Fennel; Kamloops; Morden; Primrose; and Sackville

3rd (Canadian) EG: HM Ships Saskatchewan; Skeena; Prince Rupert; Bittersweet; Eyebright; Mayflower; La Malbaie; Napanee; Pictou and Rimouski

4th EG: HM Ships Winchelsea; Bayntun; Foley; Helmsdale; Abelia; Asphodel; Clover and Pennywort

4th (Canadian) EG: HM Ships Hotspur; Churchill; Brandon; Orillia; Woodstock; Restigouche; Amherst; Nasturtium; Trillium and Collingwood

6th (Canadian) EG: HM Ships Nene; Tweed; Waskesieu; Calgary; Camrose; Edmundton; Chambly; Lunenburg; Prescott; and Snowberry

7th EG: HM Ships Vansittart; Versatile; Vidette; Highlander; Chelmer; Loosestrife; Pink; Sunflower and Kenilworth Castle

21st EG: HM Ships Saladin; Scimitar; Shikari; and Skate

24th EG: HM Ships Dianella; Lotus; Poppy; and Starwort

39th EG: HM Ships Rochester; Londonderry; Scarborough; Tavy; Azalea; Balsam; Geranium; and Mignonette

Unallocated (Royal Navy): HM Ships Duncan; Sabre; Lagan; Anguilla; Berkeley Castle; Carisbrooke Castle; and Hadleigh Castle

Unallocated (Royal Canadian Navy): HM Ships Kooteney; Dunver; Rosthern; Arvida; Dauphin; Wetaskiwin; Ottawa; Dianthus; Summerside; New Westminster; and Kitchener

HMS Foxglove (guardship)

HMS Philante (escort training yacht)

Examination Service: 5 trawlers and drifters

6 Minesweeping drifters; 6 tugs; 18 miscellaneous vessels; 1 ASR trawler (at Killybegs)

January 1945:

1st EG: HM Ships Inman; Clover; Dianella; Lotus; Poppy; Starwort; and Tintagel Castle

1st (Canadian) EG: HM Ships Hallowell; Royal Mount; Arnprior; Chambly; Fennel; Frontenac; Giffard; and Orangeville

2nd (Canadian) EG: HM Ships Capilano; Longueuil; Asbestos; Kamloops; Kincardine; and Norsyd

3rd (Canadian) EG: HM Ships Kokanee; Seacliff; St Thomas; Stellarton; Trillium; Forest Hill; and Riviere du Loup

4th (Canadian) EG: HM Ships Wentworth; Grace Bay; Beauharnois; Bowmanville; Petrolia; Whitby; Atholl; and North Bay

5th (Canadian) EG: HM Ships Runnymede; St Stephen; Hespeler; Huntsville; Lachine; Longbranch; and New Westminster

6th EG: HM Ships New Waterford; Teme; Grou; Outremont; Waskesieu; Loch Achanalt; Loch Morlich; and Cape Breton

6th (Canadian) EG: HM Ships Eastview; Lauzon; Cobourg; Peterborough; St Lambert; and Tillsonburg

7th (Canadian) EG: HM Ships Lanark; Cap de La Madelaine; Collingwood; Coppercliff; Hawkesbury; Owen Sound; and Parry Sound

8th (Canadian) EG: HM Ships Stonetown; Guelph; Leaside; Poundmaker; Edmundston; and Humberstone

9th (Canadian) EG: HM Ships Stormont; Swansea; St John*; Monnow*; Nene*; Pt Colborne*; and Loch Alvie (* loaned to Plymouth)

10th EG (loaned to Portsmouth): HM Ships Bayntun; Braithwaite; Foley; Helmsdale; Loch Eck; and Loch Dunvegan

10th (Canadian) EG (in Canada): HM Ships Antigonish; Charlottetown; Magog; Springhill; Strettler; and Toronto

11th (Canadian) EG (in Canada): HM Ships Gatineau; Kootenay; Ottawa; Restigouche; Chaudiere; Qu'Appelle; St Laurent; and Saskatchewan

20th EG: HM Ships Bahamas; Pitcairn; Sarawak; Somaliland; Tortola; and Tavy

23rd EG: HM Ships Loch Gorm; Loch Scavaig; Barbados; Montserrat; Nyasaland; and Papua

25th (Canadian) EG: HM Ships Joliette; La Hulloise; Orkney; Ste Therese; and Thetford Mines

26th (Canadian) EG: HM Ships Beacon Hill; Jonquiere; Montreal; New Glasgow; and Ribble

27th (Canadian) EG (in Canada): HM Ships Meon; Ettrick; Coaticook; La Salle; and Levis

30th EG (loaned to Portsmouth): HM Ships Caister Castle; Kenilworth Castle; Launcestown Castle; Pevensey Castle; and Portchester Castle

Base Ship: HMS Foxglove

Escort Training: HMS Philante and PC 74

Unallocated: HMS Nasturtium

Miscellaneous: 5 tugs; 3 yachts; 12 harbour craft and 1 ASR trawler (stationed at Killybegs)

June 1945:

1st EG: HM Ships Chelmer; Inman; Lotus; Poppy and Tintagel Castle

4th (Canadian) EG: HM Ships Atholl; Beauharnois; Bowmanville; Glace Bay; Petrolia; Whitby; and Wentworth

5th (Canadian) EG: HM Ships Runnymede; Lachute; St Stephen; West York; and Hespeler

6th (Canadian) EG: HM Ships Eastview; Lauzon; Peterborough; St Lambert; Tillsonburg; and Cobourg

9th (Canadian) EG: HM Ships Renetang; Fergus; Halifax; Chilliwack; Fredericton; and Thorlock

16th EG (Canadian): HM Ships Antigonish; Charlottetown; Kirkland Lake; Matane; and Stettler

Base Ship: HMS Foxglove

Unallocated: HM Ships Caister Castle; Kenilworth Castle; Launceston Castle; Pevensey Castle; and Portchester Castle

The above lists do not include ships of the United States Navy which operated out of Londonderry. Most of these were destroyer escorts (DEs). It has not proved possible to obtain a definitive listing of USN vessels based in, or calling at, the city during the war but the following has been compiled with the assistance of the Destroyer Escort Sailors' Association:

US Ships Arc; Amesbury; Bates; Blair; Blessman; Borum; Brough; Buckley; Bunch; Burke; Burrows; Camp; Howard D Crow; [Chase]; Donnell; Ebert; Enright; Fogg; Foss; Gandy; Daniel F Griffin; Hammamm; Harveson; Hopping; Hurst; [George W Ingram]; Jacob Jones; Joyce; Kirkpatrick; Charles Lawrence; Leopold*; Alexander J Luke; Maloy; Marchant; [Mills]; Oswald; Paine; Robert E Peary; Peterson; Pettit; Poole; Powell; Ramsden; Reeves; Rich; Richey; Ricketts; [Rudderow]; Sellstrom; Sims; Slater; Spangenberg; Sturtevant; US Navy (non-DEs) Albatros**; Dallas; Madison; Roper; Sturtevant***; Wilkes; Melville; Restless; Temptress; Courage; Surprise; Saucy; Spry; Fury; Impulse; Ready

The ships operating from the city were supported by a large number of other vessels. As well as the three yachts which successively carried the name *Ferret* and the guardship *Foxglove*, there were minesweepers, boom defence vessels, target-towing vessels, ferries, radar calibration vessels, auxiliary patrol vessels and a range of other vessels. Most of these were requisitioned for the war's duration and several were of foreign origin; there were seized French ships as well as Belgian and Norwegian vessels.

Employed on anti-submarine duties were the trawlers *Ayrshire*, *Le Tiger* and *St Cathan* in addition to the trawlers listed in the tables.

On minesweeping duties were the French ships *Beluga*, *Corsaire* and *Pax*, as well as the *Chapelizod*, and the trawler *Claribelle* and the drifters *John & Nora*, *Merbreeze* and *Nairnside*.

Auxiliary patrol vessels were the yachts *Haifa* and *Peter Pan*. The yacht *Onora*, which served as HMS *Ferret* in 1945 was also used for much of the war as an auxiliary patrol vessel.

Harbour defence patrol craft were the yachts *Altona* and *Wagtail*. The latter, formerly the *Firefly*, also served as HMS *Ferret* for a time.

* torpedoed and sunk en route to Derry.

** first US ship to arrive

*** first destroyer of the name; the second Sturtevant, a DE, also came to Derry.

Examination service vessels were the yacht *Bluebird*, also used as a balloon tender, the trawler *Junco*, also used for target-towing, the French tug *La Pernelle*, the drifter *Norfolk County*, and the French pilot vessel *Pouyer-Quertier*. The yacht *Clarinda* is included in the earlier tables.

Target-towing vessels were the Belgian trawler *Adronie Camiel*, also used as a ferry, and the French tugs *Pinguin*, *Pintade* and *Servannaise*.

Calibration was the task of the yachts *Dunlin*, *Hiniesta* and *St Adrien*, the Belgian drifter *Sophie-Francois*, the Norwegian drifter *Utvaer* and the pilot vessel *Prudence*.

Boom defence was carried out by the trawlers *Carabineer* and *Sunrise* while the drifter *Fragrant*, the yacht *Grey Mist*, the French ship *Notre Dame de Lourdes* and the *Senga* were harbour service vessels.

Ferries were the Norwegian ship *Sandvikthorn* and the Belgian trawler *Andre Monique* and the tug *Cervia* provided a rescue tug service while the *Robert Hastie*, a trawler provided the air-sea rescue service from Killybegs in County Donegal.

Appendix 3

BIBLIOGRAPHY

Bardon, Jonathan: A History of Ulster (Belfast, 1992)

Barnett, Correlli: Engage the Enemy more Closely – the Royal Navy in the Second World War (London, 1991)

Barton, Brian: The Blitz – Belfast in the War Years (Belfast, 1989)

Beesly, Patrick: Very Special Intelligence: The Story of the Admiralty's Operational Intelligence Centre, 1939–1945 (London, 1977)

Carroll, Joseph T: Ireland in the War Years 1939–1945 (Newton Abbot, 1975)

Destroyer Escort Sailors Association (Ed): Trim but Deadly, Volume I (Paducah, KY 1987);
Trim but Deadly, Volume II (Paducah, KY 1989);
Trim but Deadly, Volume III (Paducah, KY 1993)

Doherty, Richard: Wall of Steel – The history of the 9th (Londonderry) Heavy Anti-Aircraft Regiment, Royal Artillery (SR) (Limavady, 1988);
The Sons of Ulster – Ulstermen at War from the Somme to Korea (Belfast, 1992);
Clear the Way! – A History of the 38th (Irish) Brigade, 1941–47 (Dublin, 1993)

Fisk, Robert: In Time of War – Ireland, Ulster and the Price of Neutrality 1939–45 (London, 1983)

Gibson-Harries, Derrick: Life-line to Freedom – Ulster in the Second World War (Lurgan, 1990)

Kelly, Mary Pat: Home Away from Home – The Yanks in Ireland (Belfast, 1994)

Kemp, Paul: Convoy Protection – The Defence of Seaborne Trade (London, 1993)

Lacy, Brian: Siege City – The story of Derry and Londonderry (Belfast, 1990)

Macintyre, Captain Donald, DSO and two Bars, DSC, RN: U-Boat Killer (London, 1956)

Nesbit, Roy Conyers: An Illustrated History of the RAF (Godalming, 1990)

Purdon, Corran: List The Bugle – Reminiscences of an Irish Soldier (Antrim, 1993)

Schull, Joseph: The Far Distant Ships: an official account of Canadian naval operations in the Second World War (Ottawa, 1961)

Smith, David J: Action Stations 7 – Military Airfields of Scotland, the North-East and Northern Ireland (Cambridge, 1983)

Spooner, Tony, DSO, DFC: Coastal Ace – The Biography of Squadron Leader Terence Malcolm Bulloch, DSO and Bar, DFC and Bar (London, 1986)

Winterbotham, F W: The Ultra Secret (London, 1974)
Sturtivant, R: The Squadrons of the Fleet Air Arm (Tonbridge, 1984)

UNPUBLISHED SOURCES

Chavasse, E H: Business in Great Waters – War memories of a semi-sailor
Jeffery, Keith: Canadian Sailors in Londonderry: A Study in Civil-Military Relations

ADMIRALTY FILES
(Public Record Office; Ruskin Avenue; Kew; Richmond; Surrey)

ADM1/12769; 13150
ADM116/4386; 4520; 4598; 4640; 4644; 4645; 4651 & 4745
ADM186/799 (Naval Staff History: Second World War: Home Waters and the Atlantic; Vol I Sep 1939 – 8 Apr 1940)
ADM186/802 (German Naval History Series: The U-boat War in the Atlantic, 1939–1941)
ADM199/423; 631; 689; 1200 & 1392
ADM205/27: Washington Convoy Conference, March 1943
ADM234/370 (Naval Staff History: Battle Summary No 51; Convoy and Anti-Submarine Warfare Reports)
ADM234/578 (Naval Staff History: Defeat of the Enemy Attack on Shipping, 1939–1945: A study of policy and operations, Vol Ia)

CABINET FILES
(PRO, Kew)

CAB 86/1 (War Cabinet – Battle of the Atlantic Committee)
CAB 86/2 (War Cabinet – Anti-U-boat Warfare);

AIR MINISTRY FILES
(PRO, Kew)

AIR16/398: Fighter Command: Air Defence of Northern Ireland
AIR 27: various Operations Record Books of Coastal Command squadrons based in the north-west (with thanks to David Hill and Ernie Cromie)
AIR27/2252: Operations Record Book, 920 Balloon Squadron
AIR 41/47 (RAF in the Maritime War – Vol III Atlantic and Home Waters)

WAR OFFICE FILES
(PRO, Kew)

W0166/1172: War diary, Headquarters, Northern Ireland District (G Branch) 1939–1940.

W0166/1349: War diary, Londonderry Garrison, 1941
W0166/6869: War diary, Londonderry Garrison, 1942
W0166/9867: War diary, Londonderry Town Major, Oct–Dec 1942
W0166/13713: War diary, Londonderry Town Major, 1943
W0166/16279: War diary, Londonderry Town Major, 1944
W0166: war diaries of Anti-Aircraft Command; 12th AA Division; 3 AA Brigade; and all HAA/LAA Regiments stationed in Londonderry GDA; also 9th (Londonderry) HAA Regiment, RA (SR) September to November 1939 and October 1944 to May 1945
W0169: war diaries of RHQ, 9th (Londonderry) HAA Regiment, RA (SR); 24 and 25 HAA Batteries in Middle East Forces 1939–1943 & Central Mediterranean Forces 1943; also 2 AA Brigade, Tripoli 1943 & 12 AA Brigade, Italy 1943
W0170: war diaries of RHQ, 9th (Londonderry) HAA Regiment, RA (SR); 24 and 25 HAA Batteries in Italy 1944; also 66 AA Brigade 1944 (to August)

DEPARTMENT OF THE NAVY (WASHINGTON, DC)
US Naval United Kingdom Bases in World War II
Londonderry, North Ireland (Base I)
United States Navy and Marine Corps Bases, Overseas (Ed: Coletta & Bauer; Greenwood Press, Conn)
Guide to United States Naval Administrative Histories of World War II (Naval History Division; Department of the Navy)

Appendix 4

ACKNOWLEDGEMENTS

For their assistance in the writing and production of this book I would like to thank the following:

Bryan McCabe of Greystone Books for his support and encouragement and for the high standard of the final publication.

The Department of Photographs of the Imperial War Museum for their guidance in researching illustrations for the book; the Department of Printed Documents of the same museum for their help; the Trustees of the Imperial War Museum for permission to reproduce photographs in the book.

The staff of the Reading and Search Rooms of the Public Record Office, Kew for their assistance and patience and the Keeper of the Public Record Office for permission to quote from documents held in the PRO.

The Naval History Division, Department of the Navy, Washington DC, USA.

Dr Keith Jeffery of the University of Ulster for permission to use his 'Canadian Sailors in Londonderry: A Study in Civil-Military Relations.'

The Royal Air Force Museum, Hendon.

Colonel K G F Chavasse, DSO and Bar for allowing me to quote from his late brother Evelyn's account of his wartime service, Business in Great Waters: war memories of a semi-sailor.

David Hill and Ernie Cromic of the Ulster Aviation Society for all their help.

Weidenfeld and Nicolson for permission to quote from Captain Donald Macintyre's book U-boat Killer.

Jim Mullen, research officer, Derry City Council for his assistance and Tommy Conaghan for his help in compiling the Roll of Honour.

I must also acknowledge the assistance of all those individuals who provided information for the book, and whose names will be found in the text, or who gave me their support along the way. Without them this book would not have been possible.

As always I appreciate the patient support and understanding of my wife, Carol, and my children, Joanne, James and Catríona, as I researched and wrote this book.

Richard Doherty
March 1995

Appendix 5

ROLL OF HONOUR

ROYAL NAVY

Tel/Gnr P H C Bailey
Stkr (1st Cl) D Bradley
CPO J Brennan
S/man J Doherty
R/O D Duffy
Stkr S M Edgar
Cook J Hutchinson
Stkr H McIntyre
A Maker
Stkr A Rankin
Ch/ERA E T Starrett
A/B D C Stewart
Stkr M E Warren

ROYAL MARINES

Marine J A Smith
Marine J Traynor

ARMY

L/Cpl A J Anderson
L/Cpl A S Anderson
Gnr D Barnhill
Fus J Berry
Sgt S E Blake
Fus F Bogue
Cpl H Boyle
Fus R Bradley
Pte P Brown
Fus S Burke
Sgm T L Burke
Fus J Campbell
WO II (CSM) W Campbell
Fus W Campbell
Fus J Carlin
L/Cpl E D Carruthers
Pte J Cavanagh
Fus L Cavanagh
Sgm W Cavanagh
Cpl E Coates
Pte E Cochrane
L/Cpl T Conley
Pte J Cooke
Sgt H Cooper
Fus J Coyle
Sgt J Coyle
Spr P Coyle
Cpl W Coyle
WO II (CSM) R G Cross
Fus F Daly
Pte A Doherty
Fus B Doherty
L/Cpl D Doherty
Fus H Doherty
Fus J Doherty
Cpl J Douglas
L/Cpl W J Douglas
Cpl L England
Fus D Feeney
Fus P Feeney
Sgt B W Fenton
Piper W E M Fitzgerald
Fus G Forrest
L/Cpl A Galbraith
Cpl C Gallagher
Pte J Gallagher
L/Sgt J Gilmour
L/Cpl P Gough
L/Cpl J Gourley
Cpl R Gray

Fus E Greene
Fus J Greene
Sgt W A Griffiths
Rfn C Hamilton
Gnr R Hamilton
Fus M Hasson
Fus J J Hastings
Fus A Hegarty
Cpl W J Hegarty
Cpl H Hiscox
Gdsm L Hutchman
L/Cpl A Jackson
Dvr W J Jarvis
Rfn W J Jenkins
L Judd
L/Sgt W Kane
Fus W Kane
Gnr L A Kavanagh
Sgt A Kelly
Fus H Kelly
Gnr J Kelly
Fus W Kelly
Cpl W Kerr
Sgt T A King
Sgt W King
Rfn J J Lafferty
Fus P Larkin
Fus J Laughlin
Fus J C S Livingstone
L/Sgt B Lowry
Cpl R Lowry
Sgt M Lynch
Fus J Lynch
Fus H Maguire
Rfn J Mallett
Fus E F Martin
Rfn H V Martin
Fus J T Martin
Cpl S Martin
L/Bdr J R D Mark
Cpl R Moffatt
Fus E Mooney
Fus W Mooney
Rfn J Mullan
Fus T Mullan
Bdr N Murray
Fus H McArthur
Fus D McAteer
Fus H McAteer
Fus J McCallion
Fus J McCandless
L/Cpl P McCann
Gnr T McCarter
Fus P McCauley
Fus P C McCauley
Fus D McCloskey
Lt F D P McCorkell
Gnr S McCormick
Fus J McCullagh
Fus J McCutcheon
Sgt W McDaid
Fus J McDermott
Fus M McFadden
L/Cpl S McFeeters
Fus J McGaughey
Fus T McGaughey
Fus C McGilloway
Fus W G McGowan
Fus J McGrillis
Fus S J McKeary
Fus J J McKeown
Sgt W J McKibben
Fus T McLaughlin
Fus J McManus
Fus F McNamee
Pte W Nash
Fus J C Nelson
Rfn J H Nelson
Pte G Nicell
Fus G Nixon
L/Cpl J Norton
Pte H Oford
Pte J Orr
Fus J O'Brien
Gnr T P O'Bryan
Pte J O'Donnell
L/Cpl P O'Hagan
L/Cpl H O'Kane
Gnr E O'Neill
Pte J J O'Neill
L/Cpl E Parkhill
L/Cpl J Patterson
WO II (CSM) A Penfold
L/Bdr W S Peoples
Cpl L Pickering
Pte R Porter

Gnr T Porter
Sgt J Pring
P Purcell
L/Sgt F Quinn
Sgt R Rainey
L/Bdr J Ree
Cpl E A Reid
L/Cpl R A Reid
Fus M Reilly
Sgt E Reynolds
Sgt W A Rosborough
Fus W J Ross
Fus C Ruffell
Pte M D Ruffell
Fus J Scullion
Gnr J Shiels
Cpl M Simms
Fus C Smith
Lt A McI Smyth
Gnr J R W Smyth
Fus J J Stevenson
Fus J Tate
Fus J Tracey
Fus G Turnbull
Fus H Tyre
Fus R Walls
Cpl R Walker
Capt F G Webster
Tpr A Weeks
Sgt H Weir
Rfn W Willis
L/Cpl F Wilkinson
L/Bdr A Williams
Gdsm H Williams
Fus P Wilson
Sgt J Wray
Pte W Wray
Fus B Wright
Sgt W J Wright
Rfn D Wylie
Fus E F Zammit

ROYAL AIR FORCE

F/O S Austin
Sgt E H McK Barr
Sgt J Boyd
Sgt J Cahill
F/Sgt S E Campbell
Sgt J L Davis
A/c J R Douglas
Sgt T B Duffy
P/O A W Dunn
WO W Harvey
Sgt D Hetherington
Sgt W J Hetherington
F J Mason
Sgt P Miller
P/O S C Morrison
Sgt T F McClay
F/Sgt W McDermott
P/O J G McKinnon
J McNeary
Cpl G Niven
F/Lt F J Perry
LA/c E M Reid
P/O M C Reid
Sgt W Rodgers
T D Siddons
P/O S Smyth
Sgt J D Stewart
W/Cdr R Wilson
Sgt R G Young

MERCHANT NAVY

D Buchanan
G Crawford
R Gallagher
D H Heaney
W Logue
J Lyttle
J C McCafferty
J F O'Kane
M Rogan
D Senior
W F Strunks

The following also died on active service but their branches of service and ranks are unknown:

A Borland
S Carson
D Crowe
R J L Devine

R Dinsmore
R Johnston
H Miller
I Mitchell
T J A M O'Connell
M H Tynte

Appendix 6

SERGEANT William V Clipsham, who was charged with the manslaughter of Dungiven bus driver Albert Rodden on 17 April 1942, appeared before a general court martial, the highest military court under American law. Clipsham was accused of shooting Rodden with a machine-gun. The scout-car driver, Private Thomas de Felice, said in evidence that Rodden, whose bus was in the line of vehicles that made up the convoy, appeared determined not to allow the scout car, the last in the convoy, to pass. De Felice made four unsuccessful attempts to pass the bus. Private John J Fraula, a passenger in the scout car, said the bus obstructed the car for about a mile and when the scout car drew abreast both vehicles were travelling at such a speed that he thought a crash was inevitable. The scout car was forced into the kerb and Fraula was thrown off balance. Corporal Looney, second-in-command of the scout car, stated that at no time did Clipsham stand behind the car's forward machine-gun. Second-Lieutenant P C Madeira, the escort commander, testified that he had ordered that the machine-gun should be 'half-loaded': this meant that the gunner would need to make at least one movement to fire the weapon. Two American war correspondents who had been with the convoy also gave evidence. Robert G Nixon, said

> he noticed the bus moving into the convoy in front of the rear scout car. [He] was surprised at the action of the bus driver as the convoy was proceeding at between 40 and 45 miles per hour. The two cars seemed to jockey for position and the bus continued to block the road until it went out of control and smashed into the concrete blocks. When the scout car drew up [Nixon] went up to the accused and asked him if there had been any shooting. Accused replied that a gun had gone off, but he did not know where. At times there was oncoming traffic on the road.

Other witnesses supported Fraula and de Felice's evidence: an escort motorcyclist said that he had drawn up alongside the bus and asked the driver to let the scout car pass; the driver had told him to 'stay behind' and motioned him to do so. On the car's fourth attempt to pass the motorcyclist said that the bus had moved out, forcing the car over to the far kerb. Clipsham told much the same story but denied that he had been holding the machine-gun at the time of the incident: he had, he said, had both hands over his head trying to wave Rodden over. Afterwards he had examined the gun and found that three rounds had been fired.

Technical evidence was given by Corporal Picariello, a weapons instructor. On the Monday after the incident he had examined the machine-gun and discovered that, if half-loaded, it would go off after being tapped a few times. 'It was,' he said, 'normal practice to tap this make of gun to see if it was defective.' An Ordnance Maintenance Department technical sergeant, who had also examined the gun, gave his opinion that the weapon was defective and that a sharp knock could have caused it to fire. The prosecution, in its concluding summary, maintained that Clipsham was responsible for the weapon, that any negligence was his fault, and that the evidence was strong enough to show that he was the only one in the scout car who could have 'touched the gun off'. The defence submitted that the charge had not been proved, and that evidence had been brought to show that the gun was defective. After the court had retired for a short time to consider its verdict the president announced that all seven members were unanimous that Sergeant Clipsham was not guilty of the charge brought against him.